Angels, Vampires & Douche Bags

CARLA COLLINS

Angels, Vampires & Douche Bags

BURMANBOOKS

Dedication

I would like to dedicate this book to
my beautiful, beloved hairdresser
and second mom, Mena Spina.
She was a rare angel who simply wasn't
on this earth for nearly enough time.
I miss you Spiner, but I know that
you are watching over me every day.

Acknowledgments

There are several people to whom I owe a debt of gratitude roughly the size of Roman Polanski's bail bond.

I would like to thank my remarkable mom Rosemarie for her love and guidance. She is my hero, my mentor and my kindred spirit. She has always been my biggest fan despite the fact that lately I have begun whimsically introducing her as my "birth mother."

I want to thank my awesome brother Rick (aka: Pal) for his unwavering belief in me and for always encouraging me to write a book. I also want to thank him in advance for any of his best jokes that I may have stolen and passed off as my own in this book.

I wish to thank my extraordinary, handsome and inspirational husband Ty for his unconditional love and support; and for putting up with me for weeks on end as I sat sequestered up in our tiny office wearing the same pair of red monkey pajamas and rarely showering. That must have been straight up sexy for him!

I am grateful to my genius publisher Sanjay Burman for inventing the new subgenre of "comedic motivational" book, and for giving me this incredible opportunity.

Another gratitude shout-out goes to my brilliant, British editor Drew Tapley who took such wonderful care of my baby and who was an absolute dream to work with. Plus, I automatically added a good twenty points to his IQ when I heard his English accent.

To my dog and muse Buster, who sat patiently at my feet the entire time I wrote this book.

Finally, I want to thank my exceptional, amazing and crazy friends. They are all angels (well, maybe a couple are vampiresque), and I am beyond blessed to have them in my life.

Table of Contents

Preface

The number *three* packs one hell of a punch. It's a very spiritual and mystical number. From the Holy Trinity to the three witches, it is evident that three is a magical number. Examples of the number three abound in grammar, literature, legislature and science. Body, mind and soul; past, present and future; yin, yang and Tao—the list is endless.

There are three primary colors, three true norths, three types of reasoning, and three phases of the moon; not to mention that we are three-dimensional beings inhabiting this earth, and we do things in threes so that they will manifest in our physical realm. Three is the first number representing completion, and the first to which the meaning "all" was attributed.

The number three is also essential in comedy, with "the rule of three" used for humorous anecdotes: The first two jokes in a list are routine, but the third represents the big punch line. The number three is also prevalent in the rhythm and cadence of comedy. For example: a priest, a rabbi and a centaur walk into a bar....

More importantly, there are Three Stooges, three Charlie's Angels, three good Star Wars movies; the 80s band The Police was a trio, and Rush (of course) is known as the Holy Triumvirate.

As a woman of French descent, I can also tell you that the French flag has three colors, the fleur-de-lys three points, and the popular French expression: *jamais deux sans trois* translates to "all things come in threes" (which may also translate into me eventually having a third husband).

And the list goes on. Every man's fantasy is a three-way, celebrities often die in threes, and ancient wisdom postulates how events that come in threes are worth noticing... like orgasms, for instance.

So, either the number three has a kick-ass publicist, or there really is something to this triangular number. Sadly, the only time the rule of three doesn't apply is in the context of body parts. Those tend to come in ones and twos. Maybe that's what's wrong with us. Who couldn't use a third eye... or breast?

Well, after noticing the power and omnipresence of the number three in virtually all aspects of life (heaven, man, and earth), I decided to throw my own hat-trick into the ring. I have come up with the definitive triad for our times: angels, vampires and douche bags. It is my firm belief that every person, place or thing falls into one of these three categories. Since I am always immediately on a trend like a bruise on a stripper, I humbly present the latest threesome to bless the written page.

(*Note:* stories about angels appear throughout this book, even in the DOUCHE BAGS section. That's just how angels are!)

Angels, Vampires & Douche Bags

PART I

Angels

an·gel [**eyn**-j*uhl*]
——*noun*

1. one of a class of spiritual beings; a celestial attendant of God.
2. a conventional representation of such a being, in human form, with wings, usually in white robes.
3. a person having qualities generally attributed to an angel, as beauty, purity or kindliness.

"The reason angels can fly is because they take themselves lightly."
—G.K. CHESTERTON

My definition is somewhat more unconventional. I define an angel as someone who loves you unconditionally; someone who inspires and moves you; someone who repeatedly saves your ass.

I'm hoping to expand your concept of angels. Forget the archetype of the traditional messenger of God who is present in most religions—the celestial body sporting massive wings and a shiny, golden halo. I'm not discounting this heavenly creature. If you've had the good fortune of spotting one and you weren't high on magic mushrooms at the time, more power to you. My focus is on the earthbound variety of angel.

An angel can be someone you've known all your life, like a relative or a dear friend. There are also angels who travel along your path for only a limited time. They may just be seasonal angels, kind of like a Shamrock Shake. They appear in your life just when you need them the most, and then seem to drift away.

There are also random angels or one-offs as I call them. I'm not suggesting that a one-night stand will necessarily produce an angelic figure in your life, but there are many strangers we meet by chance and never see again, who, with a simple and kind gesture or a few well-placed bons mots, have a profound impact on us.

There appear to be more angels than flavors of Baskin-Robbins ice cream—the guardian angels who don red berets and keep the streets and cyberspace safe; the notorious Hell's Angels who drive Harleys and are often covered in more ink than Obama's health care bill; Angel Perfume;

and angel investors. I once knew a former stripper who went by the stage moniker "Angel Cakes," which brings an entirely new meaning to the 90s television show *Touched by an Angel*.

Angels aren't just found in the kingdom of Homo sapiens. Nature, animals, music, food, laughter, geographical locations, and vibrators can all be imbued with angelic properties. For example, the ocean has always been an angel to me. It's healing, energizing, inspiring, calming and invigorating. The ocean is like a $5 Thai hooker... anything you want it to be.

For some, a long hot bath, a deep-tissue massage, and a glass of Pinot Noir are higher on the angelic food chain than a flushed, tubby cherub sporting a bow and arrow.

My shortlist of angels includes, but is not limited to, a young German writing partner, a psychic colon therapist, a beloved hairdresser, a Russian limo driver, a wise Wiccan, a reformed party girl who swears like a seasoned truck driver, a couple of nudists, rescue dogs, uncontrollable laughter, and coconut mojitos.

Interestingly, if you google the word *angels*, the first listing you'll find is the official site of the Anaheim Angels baseball team. Maybe this isn't that far off the mark. Baseball has certainly been an angel to many players and their fans; and has also prevented several men from premature ejaculation throughout the years.

Chapter 1

Spirits in the Maternal World

"It's not easy being a mother. If it was easy, fathers would do it."
—THE GOLDEN GIRLS

If you're lucky, the first angel you meet and fall in love with is your mother. This was certainly the case for me. In fact, for the longest time I thought my mom Rosemarie was my soul mate. It's always been tough for the men in my life to compete with her. She's brilliant, beautiful, hilarious, successful, and can out-drink any fella. She's very nonjudgmental, extremely supportive and wise. How could I not have a crush on her? Rosie has always been a *bonne vivante*, yet still maintains a sweet innocence about her. Not long ago, I remember her telling me that her colleague Bill had just completed AA and was now allowed to drink only white wine. Really, mom? Do other alcoholics know about this loophole?

I come from a large and matriarchal French-Canadian family. Because my mom has so many sisters, I have always been surrounded by wonderful, strong and loving female family members. Growing up was like being a part of some kind of Bizarro World Lilith Fair, but with fewer hairy armpits. More accurately, it was like a very special episode of *The View* with noisy, expressive French-Canadian women talking over each other, and without the annoying, extreme right-wing opinions of Elisabeth Hasselbeck.

I was raised in Sault Ste. Marie, a small steel town in

Northern Ontario, Canada. I like to joke that there is a sign on the way into the city that reads: "Have fun in 'The Soo.' You'll be the first!" The thing is, I did have fun there. Even though there was snow on the ground ten months of the year, it was a warm and nurturing city to grow up in. I had a fabulous childhood (things didn't start to come undone in my life, like a cheap department store bra, until later on). Sure, it was a tad isolated. In fact, the first dude I ever made out with was my cousin George. Hey, I know what you're thinking—Carla, how could you kiss a guy named George? The Great White North isn't all that different from the deep, Deep South. We're just better at hockey... and less racist.

Because my mom was a high school teacher, I spent most of my pre-Kindergarten days with my Auntie Alice, one of my mom's elder sisters. Auntie Alice is an incredible angel with a lovely, soft demeanor and the patience of Job. To be fair, my mother eventually became a wonderful cook; but when I was a kid, to say Rosie was domestically-challenged would be an understatement. She's a wonderful mother, but, at that time, she was retarded in the kitchen. Imagine my awe when I first began frequenting Auntie Alice's house and witnessed her making donuts... from scratch! I thought she was a superhero with unearthly powers.

We lived with my maternal *mémère* (grandmother) until I was almost six-years-old. I adored my mémère. Here's the kicker—she was nearly fifty-years-old when she gave birth to her youngest daughter, my mom. That's right; mémère was born in the nineteenth century, but she was truly a renaissance woman who made all her children's clothes, was a gourmet chef, and she played the piano by ear. Sadly, I didn't have many years with her because she passed when I was only eight. I was devastated and my mom wasn't the same for a very long time. They were so close that my heart would break whenever I watched my mom dialing mémère's phone number months after she died. The two of them spoke every day, just like mom and I do now.

Even though I only had a brief time on this earth with my grandmother, she had a greater impact on my life than anyone else to this day. I like to think that she is still with me, watching over me like a guardian angel with white hair and dentures.

Mémère and I frequently slept together in the same room, and we talked all night. She said I was like a little old lady, and spoke to me like I was an adult. I'd watch mémère prepare Christmas food baskets for underprivileged families. She never officially had a "professional job," but she made a career out of doing non-stop charity work. She also taught me that all good deeds should be done anonymously, without glory but with a great deal of pride. Mémère was also very political and campaigned tirelessly for the Canadian Liberal Party.

For decades, mémère (then later my mom's elder sisters) ran the Joan of Arc Bingo, a charitable organization responsible for the funding of the French Catholic church in Sault Ste. Marie. Over the years, these women raised a great deal of money and donated it to community charities, but I always questioned naming a game of chance after someone who was burned at the stake. What does that say about your odds of winning? Or even getting out of the Bingo parlor alive?

A while ago, I tried my hand at bingo back in The Soo

and immediately came to the conclusion that I must have been adopted because I have no skills at all at this sport. I just remember suffering from extreme anxiety and smoke inhalation trying to manage my solo card while my aunts wielded what looked like Swiss Army dabbers—effortlessly playing thirty cards each.

The bingo talisman was also a source of confusion to me. Most charms are rooted in folklore or mythology. In Ireland and abroad, a four-leaf clover signals good fortune, with the traditional three leaves representing the Holy Trinity and the rare fourth symbolizing God's grace. The yin yang is, of course, the ancient Chinese metaphysical concept of two opposites. But how the hell did the furry troll doll become the patron saint of Bingo parlors? Almost every hardcore dabber in the place was surrounded by a rainbow army of tacky, three-inch-high smiling rodent monsters with Don King's lid. How does a disheveled troll equal luck? If you really think an unkempt, filthy creature who spends most of his time in a ditch under a bridge will increase your odds of winning at bingo, why not just bring my Uncle Louis into the hall. Maybe get him to play a couple of cards for ya?

My point is, no matter what the circumstances, whoever your early childhood education angels were, embrace them and be thankful for them. No, they weren't perfect or divine; they were human and flawed. As my comedian friend Amy Anderson says, "No matter what your relationship was with your mother, be grateful for her because that woman held up your big, fat, floppy head for the first six months of your life."

Under the B, beloved grandmother

"The phrase 'working mother' is redundant."

—JANE SELLMAN

One evening my mother and I were discussing the pros and cons of organized religion. I was mostly discussing the cons. I like to think that I am a highly-evolved and spiritual individual, but to me organized religion is a lot like George Dubya's foreign policy and the Ford Explorer: Nice attempts, but man-made and ultimately extremely damaging. If it's something that helps you, that's cool. It's just not my bag.

I've always questioned the Catholic Church and its doctrine. Even as a teenager, I felt that the hypocrisy was evident on many levels. For starters, I went to a Catholic school where we were taught from a very early age not to have sex before marriage. That's all fine and dandy, but why preach abstinence to all the adolescent Catholic schoolboys and then insist that the Catholic schoolgirls come to class every day dressed as strippers in knee-high socks and plaid mini-kilts with less material than Carrot Top's act? But I digress. During the aforementioned philosophical conversation with my mom, she told me a story about my French grandmother that epitomizes my mémère's goodness, open-mindedness, and her complete lack of patience for any bias or intolerance.

When my mother was ten-years-old, she and her best friend Nola were inseparable. At that time, my mom was a student at St. Ignatius, a French first-language school in The Soo. Both the church and the school had been founded by Jesuits. Back then, the parish priest was Father Isabelle,

S.J. In both Canada's official languages these initials stand for *Société de Jésus* or Society of Jesus. During Lent, the Jesuits often dispatched their best orator-priests to various parishes to present sermons during Holy Week. So it was that my mother and her little classmates were marched single file next door to the church where a visiting Jesuit priest gave new meaning to the expression "Hellfire and brimstone." During his heated sermon, the priest issued the unequivocal statement that only Catholics would go to heaven when they died; all others would burn in the everlasting fires of hell. This had such a dramatic and visceral impact on my mother that she became physically ill, and her young mind and active imagination pictured her best friend Nola surrounded by flames while Satan laughed maniacally in the background. Mom knew Nola and her family attended the Lutheran Church, and that Lutherans were something other than Catholics.

When my mother arrived home to the welcoming aroma of mémère's freshly-baked oatmeal cookies, she raced upstairs and slammed shut her bedroom door. Even in the secure and loving atmosphere of her home, she could not erase the vision of Nola burning to death. Mémère, thinking my mother was ill since it was the first time in ten years her daughter had ever passed up a cookie, went upstairs and found her youngest child crying uncontrollably and screaming, "Nola's going to hell! Nola's going to hell!" Once mémère finally discovered the reason for her daughter's hysterical outburst, she told her to wash her face, took her by the hand and marched her at breakneck speed to the church rectory. There, she banged on the door and demanded to speak to the visiting priest.

When the priest presented himself, mémère let fly a litany of one-sided arguments about the priest's ill-founded philosophy, crushing the little man with her logic and quotations from Scripture. She then demanded that he retract what she considered to be old-wives' tales from the Middle Ages. When the stunned priest tried to interrupt, she pointed her finger at him and ended her monologue with a brilliant closer: "You are a close-minded priest drowning in prejudice who does not deserve to have the letters S.J. after his name." And with that, she took my mother's hand, turned on her heel and left.

Mémère did not utter a single word on the way home, but with every step they took, her daughter silently admired her mother's strength and determination. Later as she ate her cookies, mémère's youngest child also knew that her normally gentle and unassuming mother had just taught her a lesson she would never forget. Once my mom had shared this story with me, I never forgot it either.

Friends in high places

"Realism is a bad word. In a sense everything is realistic.
I see no line between the imaginary and the real."
—FEDERICO FELLINI

My brother Rick had Bobby Arrow. My father had Torty. One of my girlfriends had Mimi and Mr. Gibbles. Most children have *an* imaginary friend, I had seventy-two. That's right, seventy-two imaginary friends! Well, some were just imaginary acquaintances; I mean, who has the time or energy.

My pretend gang was like a United Colors of Benetton

commercial that included every race, age, color and creed. My best imaginary friend was a young girl called Finney, an adorable little blonde nymph who always sported braids. Also lucky enough to be in the inner imaginary circle was Pillie, a redhead with a pixie cut and countless freckles who often grappled with her jealousy over my close relationship with Finney. Pillie could be a real bitch sometimes; she was more of an imaginary frenemy.

My imaginary posse also included Spootz: a dreamy teenage boy who had a penchant for dressing up like a musketeer, and Pan and Panned: seventy-eight-year-old identical Quaker twins. When I think back on the latter now, it's a tad creepy. WTF? Why did I have near-octogenarian twins as imaginary friends? ("OK now Carla, show me on the dolly where the bad Amish man touched you?") Jesus, it just seems like an odd entourage for a three-year-old. Not to worry, the twins were always quite sweet and grandfatherly.

There were also fringe imaginary groupies: A talking squirrel-like creature who chain-smoked; a blowsy, sweet Jamaican woman; and a chubby, slightly annoying, passive-aggressive monk; but I can't recall many of the others. I just know that I was never lonely and I always had a good-sized audience for the various bedtime variety shows I would stage every night.

My parents never discouraged me. My folks—and quite often their guests—listened patiently as I introduced my invisible amigos and regaled everyone with seemingly never-ending stories about our wacky adventures together. I've heard that many parents will set an extra place at the table for their child's imaginary friend; but with seventy-two of the little make-believe bastards running around, what the hell could my poor mother do to indulge me... rent out a hall at the Legion?

On a warm July afternoon when I was almost five, tragedy struck. As my father was backing the car out of the driveway, he ran over one of my imaginary friends. I had an apoplectic fit. I became hysterical and began screaming like a little girl... mostly because I was a little girl. I was also completely mystified as to why my father couldn't see the little guy who was now hopelessly pinned under one of the back tires. My father immediately switched gears and gently nudged the car back up the gravel lane, but it was too late. I'm not entirely clear on whether my imaginary pal was killed or just severely injured. I also don't remember his name, but he looked a lot like Simon from *Lord of the Flies*. Naturally, the Christ figure always gets it.

Mom grew so concerned about my rich and overpopulated fantasy life that she decided to broach the subject with our family doctor. Dr. Seigel chuckled and told my mom that there was absolutely no reason to worry; in fact, quite the contrary. According to him, imaginary friends were a sign of a highly intelligent and creative child. Our family doctor continued with his upbeat and reassuring dissertation on the merits of imaginary playmates until my mom interrupted him by blurting out the exact number of make-believe people frequenting her daughter's head: "But she has seventy-two!" With this new information, the good doctor turned quite pale, and, mouth slightly agape, stood motionless and speechless save for the rapid blinking of his eyes. After what seemed like an interminably long silence, he simply muttered, "I see," and instructed my mom to take my temperature on a regular basis.

I don't know when my surreal mates began to disappear, but I think it was probably around the time my little brother Rick was a toddler. Rick became my world and pulled focus from the bogus. I never again saw any of my pretend friends. However, throughout my adult years I have had several imaginary agents.

Perhaps there was more to my invisible childhood pals than I initially gleaned. In fact, it was a discussion with my buddy James about the high volume of my imaginary friends that sparked my interest in Kabbalah. James informed me that the number *seventy-two* was quite significant to this brand of Jewish mysticism. In Kabbalah, the "72 Names of God" is a very powerful tool that helps us overcome the negative in our lives.

Many paranormal enthusiasts assert that imaginary friends are actually ghosts who can only be seen by children because they are so open and fearless. Um, if that's the case, then I was more haunted than a Stephen King hotel, and my childhood was less Hayley Mills and more Haley Joel Osment.

Others firmly believe that these pretend companions are actually guardian angels sent to guide us throughout our lives. I quite fancy this concept. However, if this is true then I suspect that in lieu of doing their job and looking out for me, my seventy-two pals have decided to make my entire life a drinking game and do a shot every time I fuck up. They must all be raging alcoholics by now.

CHAPTER 2

A Muse and Amusement

"I've actually always thought that a big laugh is really a loud noise from the soul saying, 'Ain't that the truth!'"
—QUINCY JONES

This next category of angels focuses on those who inspire us and the importance—let me rephrase that—absolute necessity of humor in our lives.

The muse has its roots in Greek mythology. These Greek goddesses who presided over the arts and sciences were the daughters of Zeus and Mnemosyne. It is believed that the Muses inspired poets, musicians and philosophers. The modern dictionary defines a muse as a force or person, especially a woman, who inspires a creative artist. For example, Uma Thurman has long been Quentin Tarantino's muse.

I think a muse is just about anything that blows your skirt up and tickles you enough to want to do something about it. I adore the word muse, and have often dreamed of becoming a professional muse myself. I rather delight in the idea of wearing long, flowing, ethereal gowns, and draping myself over a chaise longue while my mere presence inspires some wunderkind genius auteur-in-the-making to create his masterpiece.

Like any great (or mediocre) aspiring artist, my life has been stimulated by a series of muses. For instance, there's Sting. Yes, I know he's pushing sixty, but I would still ride him like a Big Wheel. His features are chiseled, his voice is haunting, and his love-making lasts longer than a Ken Burns documentary.

There's also Madonna. I'm aware that Madonna has slept with so many men that she had to marry a dude named Guy and date a fella named Jesus just so she wouldn't yell out the wrong name in bed. But just look at her staying power! I am in awe of her trailblazing and marketing skills. I respect that through yoga she has become as flexible as her morals, and I also admire her interest in Kabbalah. Remember a few years ago when Madonna took on her Hebrew name Esther? Well, not long ago, at the Kabbalah Center, I took on my Hebrew drag queen name. I am now Yum Yum Kippur. Kahlil Gibran is another muse of mine. He's the freakin' prophet. 'Nuff said!

Dance and yoga are two more of my inspirations. I took dance lessons from the age of two, yet I still look like Olive Oyl on crack out in the clubs. Yoga is one of the only activities I've discovered on this earth that is truly transformational. I love every type of yoga, except naked yoga—that shit will hurt your eyes. Seriously, the downward dog becomes the upturned starfish in no time. My latest muse is champagne. It's French, bubbly, and goes down easy... What's not to love?

I encourage you to tap into your personal muses. Whether it's men or a mentor, a superhero or a supermodel, music or a mosaic—pay attention to what moves you and move towards it more often. Muses will make you hemorrhage ideas.

On the subject of laughter, there simply isn't enough time or space to praise all of its virtues. Simply put, without laughter and humor we would all be dead inside. Victor

Borge called laughter "the closest distance between two people." Jimmy Buffet declares that "if we couldn't laugh, we would all go insane." The Kabbalists refer to it as "The Holy Laughter," and consider it the most effective form of channeling the light.

Laughter reduces stress, burns calories, strengthens the immune system, and bonds humans like nothing else does. Laughter releases endorphins, providing us with the cheapest, nonnegative side-effect drug known to mankind. Laughter brings instant joy to a world that gets off on immediate gratification. Laughter provides much-needed perspective and negates fear. Mark Twain once said that the human race has only one really effective weapon, and that is laughter.

Let's face it, laughter is like a colonic for the soul. I would like to be laughter's pimp, because I could sell that bitch to anyone.

Sometimes an orange isn't an orange

"I would especially like to re-court the Muse of poetry, who ran off with the mailman four years ago, and drops me only a scribbled note from time to time."

—JOHN UPDIKE

Tim is an artist I met while I was studying in Switzerland at the tender age of sixteen. My mother was teaching French to a group of Toronto high school students one summer in the Swiss Alps, and I was lucky enough to tag along for a couple of weeks.

Tim was a man in his late twenties who christened me his muse. After a rather innocent fling (muses are only

allowed to kiss and perhaps go to second base), Tim continued to correspond with me upon my return to Canada.
He often sent me avant-garde postcards I rarely understood
(my parents were less than thrilled when one of these cards
featured two exquisite topless Asian women spooning on a
beach).

Tim also sent me beautiful poems I understood even
less. One night, I was under the gun for a Grade 12 English
assignment. For our final project of the year we were asked
to compose a variety of poems using different styles: a
haiku, a sonnet, a ballad, and a descriptive poem—the
whole Elizabeth Barrett Browning/Alfred Lord Tennyson
nine yards. I had written most of the required poems, but
struggled to finish the descriptive verse.

It was nearly two o'clock in the morning when my mom
suggested that I abandon my attempt at an original fourth
piece of work, and simply submit one of Tim's literary mas-
terpieces along with the rest of my own verses. I was a huge
scholastic nerd and wanted to ace my English course. We
decided on one of Tim's earlier works: an extremely descriptive poem about an orange resting on a piece of velvet.
Mom's genius-idea allowed me to get some much-needed
teenage sleep.

I got an A+ on this final assignment, but the teacher
wrote "highly erotic" at the top of Tim's poem and locked
eyes with me when he handed back my assignment. I
remember thinking, "Highly erotic? Everything OK at
home, Mr. Duncan?" In fact, Mr. Duncan found the poem so
extraordinary that he published it in the school newspaper.
After enduring giggles from fellow students and looks of
horror from some of the faculty, I decided to investigate

what all the fuss was about. It took a few of the older boys at school to break down the basic imagery of Tim's *chef-d'oeuvre*. Apparently, mom and I were both too naïve to notice that the poem was actually about a clitoris.

To this day, anyone who reads the poem about the orange resting on a piece of velvet either thinks of me as a plagiarist, or a very giving lesbian lover.

Making an ash of myself

"God is a comedian, playing to an audience too afraid to laugh."
—VOLTAIRE

My second husband is named Tyrone Power Jr. My plan is to remain married to him for a while, divorce him, and marry a man with the surname "Ranger"—thus becoming Carla Power Ranger. Best. Stage Name. Ever.

Ty and I had been married for about a year when we decided to rent a townhouse in Malibu. During the utter chaos of moving, I was taping a pilot for one of my comedy idols, Jerry (*Airplane!*) Zucker, and desperately wanted to impress him. I was doing a one-woman show and wanted to bring some flyers to Mr. Zucker in the hope that he would attend my little cabaret. It was the day after we had moved to our new place, and our new home looked like the battle-front lines in Kandahar. Seriously, it was such a disaster zone with boxes, clothing and miscellaneous pieces of furniture strewn everywhere, that FEMA was nearly called in. I couldn't find a damn thing, not even a pair of panties.

I was running late and needed something to put my flyers in. I finally tripped over a small, crumpled up, ghetto-looking bag missing one of its handles, and decided it would do the trick in a pinch. The moment I tried to pick up the fragile little sack, a small burgundy box came tumbling out which I then inadvertently kicked, causing a cloud of dust to form around it. My dog Buster came over to investigate, and gently licked some of the grey dirt that had emptied out of the box. At this point, Ty walked into the room and announced, with a hint of a smile, that I shouldn't use that bag as it was tenuously holding the box that contained *some* of his late mother's ashes. Some of them? Where the hell were the rest of them? In an empty Captain Crunch box?

For the record, Ty's mother had been dead for more than two years. She had passed a few months before the two of us met. Apparently, she had requested that some of her ashes be buried in Arizona and the remainder with Ty's father. Ty just hadn't gotten around to the latter.

This new information came as a complete shock to me. I had no idea that my husband's mother had been living with us. Why did Ty leave her lying on the floor? He could have at least put her in the guest room. Needless to say, I had a mild freak-out over the fact that I had just spilled my deceased mother-in-law; not to mention that I may have let her soul escape out into the atmosphere.

Look, I'm very superstitious and I'm not entirely sure how these things work, but I figure letting mom out of the box and drop-kicking her across the living room floor wasn't good. After crossing myself, chanting Zeppelin lyrics, lighting incense and anything else I could think of to literally bless this mess, I pulled myself together long enough to gently sweep the remains of her remains back into the little burgundy container.

The next day Ty and I lovingly carried his mom's ashes to the Hollywood Forever Cemetery where she is now resting peacefully alongside her late husband. Of course, due to the fact that my dog Buster may have swallowed some of the ashes, it's quite possible that she is now also resting peacefully across our front lawn.

CHAPTER 3

Always Work with Children and Animals

"No, doll. It's not a good idea for me to write a book about raising children. That's like letting Hannibal Lecter loose in a nudist colony armed with a bottle of barbecue sauce."

—BONNIE SHORE

W.C. Fields wouldn't approve, but what the hell did he know? The persona he created was a hard-drinking egotist who hated everything. I only hate some things.

In this third category of angels, the emphasis is on the dogs and the little people in our lives... and I don't mean midgets. Children probably provide the greatest joy to most people on this earth with their candor and innocence. I adore children but don't have any of my own. Frankly, at my age I don't know whether to have a kid or date one. Seriously, no one can melt your heart or put things into perspective better than a little moppet. If only we could retain that childlike honesty and wide-eyed view of the world instead of becoming adults and letting society screw us up to the point of psychotherapy and fistfuls of Xanax.

Admittedly, I think children are the greatest thing we have going for us as humans, but I do have a couple of caveats on the subject. First of all, I'm still bewildered as to why parents of twins or triplets insist on dressing their kids in identical outfits. Is this really necessary? It's a bit too *Children of the Corn* for my liking.

Secondly, I must confess that babies make me very nervous. They are just so fragile. Sure, I love the way they smell and how unbelievably tiny their hands are, but I feel that everyone with a newborn practically forces you to hold their baby against your will. I hate this pressure. Do you know how many times I've dropped my Blackberry? Please don't shove your delicate baby into my arms like a football. The infant invariably begins to cry and then everyone knows I'm evil. Send the kids back to me when they're walking, talking, and the soft spot at the top of their head has hardened. That's when Auntie Carla should show up on the scene.

Finally, only babies should be breastfed. If your child has a learner's permit and can drive over to your breast, they're too old to still be suckling at your teat and should be immediately weaned lest you be thought of as creepy.

I also feel that during these trying financial times, babies have become the new collectibles. Clearly, women are having babies more often than they're having gas. Is this fetus frenzy in order to create a new "eggconomy"? (That's right, I coined that.) Let the baby revolution begin; it appears to be the solution to every problem. "I lost my keys." Have a baby. "I lost my job." Have a baby. "I couldn't follow the last season of *Lost.*" Have a baby. In fact, have several. I blame Octomom; she's parlaying her brood into reality-show glory. Please stop saying she looks like Angelina Jolie. She looks like a butch Steven Tyler at best.

I think my husband and I are just going to start with a nanny and see how that goes. Besides, from what I hear, when you're pregnant you can't drink, smoke, take warm baths, dye your hair or eat sushi. Um... that's basically all I do. I don't know how I'd fill my days. I'd have to take up Guitar Hero or learn Spanish.

I've always wanted to adopt, and have given some very serious thought to adopting an older child. But so far, the only thing I have adopted has been a British accent after a few glasses of Veuve Clicquot.

Of course, dog is man's best friend, but I would argue that a dog is more accurately a white woman's soul mate. Trust me, white women have an unholy dependency on canines. I think it's because we have no inner compass: no barometer or gut feelings. Every other ethnic group seems to have this gift. For example, my black girlfriends are always telling me they can "feel someone" or "vibe something." My Persian girlfriends warn me about the "evil eye." White women don't recognize a red flag until it's dunked in chloroform, shoved in their mouths and secured with duct tape. Even then we only sigh and say, "Maybe I shouldn't go out on a second date with this guy?"

This is why I need my dog Buster. He yelps or growls whenever someone unsavory approaches. I wish I wasn't so reliant on my black lab. I wish, well, I wish my vagina could bark. Imagine that? Just hearing a ferocious woof-woofwooofwoof emanating from that region? You'd think twice about going in there, wouldn't ya? My dude would be all awkward and I would have all the power. I'd say, "She just has to get used to you. Let her sniff your hand. You know, she's a rescue vagina... abused by her previous owner. Just give her a bone!"

Only a thought....

Rescuing dogs is my passion in life. We currently have two amazing adopted pooches: The aforementioned Buster the Wonder Dog, and a young Chihuahua mix called Dr. Zira who likes to sleep curled up on my crotch. That's just how she rolls!

Dogs are remarkable angels because they give us unconditional love, comfort and unimaginable joy. They are loyal and grateful healers known to reduce high blood pressure— not to mention that you can blame them for any farts in your home ("That damn dog must have gotten into something!").

There are countless stories on the news about dogs that traveled 1,600 miles in stormy weather to make their way back to their beloved owners. Dogs are able to sniff cancer in someone's leg and rescue children and the elderly from burning buildings. You never hear about a dog scamming someone out of millions of dollars in a Ponzi scheme or breaking up with someone on Facebook. And do I have to mention the fact that dogs are the animals responsible for giving us a terrific sexual position? I mean, when is the last time you ever made love giraffe style?

Having dogs is also very humbling. For the love of Zeus, how can they not be? We are required to pick up their poop on a daily basis. Mind you, I would rather clean up after my dogs than take crap from a person on any given day. The only problem is their ridiculously short lifespan. In a way, this makes dogs even more precious because they live only in their childhood.

Here's my guarantee to you. If you rescue a dog, he will rescue you back and enhance your life. Plus, they make a great combo platter with kids. Bottom line: Cherish the children and rescue dogs, not adults. You can't rescue people; they have to rescue themselves.

Shock and paw

"No animal should ever jump up on the dining room furniture unless absolutely certain that he can hold his own conversation."
—FRAN LEBOWITZ

My ex-husband Jon and I both rescued dogs. When we were married, we had a total of five canines living with us, and all our pooches were adopted from the Humane Society or various shelters in the Toronto area. In rescue order, they included: Whiskey, a beautiful Walker coon-hound Jon had before we met; Buster, my thirteen-year-old black lab-cross who still lives with me now; Big Red, a crazy hound-mix who may be part goat for all we know; Bugsy, an aging quasi-blind pug who (when he was wearing a post-operation halo) was a dead ringer for Dame Judi Dench in *Shakespeare in Love*; and Odd Job, a young hound who often worked in tandem with Big Red.

Evidently, we didn't heed the cautionary tale imparted in *Star Trek*—never be outnumbered by another species in your own home. They'll wage a coup. That's why Capt. Kirk only allowed one Vulcan on the Enterprise. Our dogs certainly ruled the house.

Buster (aka: Angel Dog) is a gentle soul who is more mature than I am (not difficult), and he is definitely the love of my life. Well, he certainly represents the longest-lasting relationship I've had with any man. There'll never be another doggie like this fella. However, Big Red always steals the show.

Red now resides with my ex-husband, as he should, considering this dog is the perfect embodiment of all men. Ironically, Big Red is not a big dog, but he is larger than life. He looks like a butterscotch sundae with freckles, and has bigger bags under his eyes than Vince Vaughn. For some reason, Big Red always looks partied out. I believe it's because of his hardcore lifestyle.

We rescued Red when he was two-years-old. His paperwork was iffy from the start, and he was listed as both a stray and a three-time surrender. The last couple brought Red back to the shelter because he had eaten two of their loveseats and an entire Lazy Boy recliner. When we first brought him home, Whiskey and Buster did not know what to make of this dog that appeared to be jacked up on coke. Red ran furiously in circles for the first forty-eight hours. He eventually simmered down, but his high-wired energy was the least of our problems.

Because he came from the mean streets, Red always feared he would go hungry, and despite ample food at mealtimes and months of training and nurturing, the damn dog ate everything. I mean EVERYTHING. All the time. You couldn't so much as gesture with a muffin in your hand because he would snatch and devour it. He was always quite wily during the holidays when he would lie down in my mom's kitchen and pretend to be asleep, just biding his time until she stepped away from the turkey. If you looked closely, you could see that he always had one eye open. Not only did Big Red polish off most of my throw pillows and several expensive pairs of Manolo Blahniks, he would actually ingest batteries, razor blades, and the occasional wooden sculpture.

One time, while we were vacationing at a friend's cottage, we returned from an evening out to find that Big Red had wolfed down a Power Bar and all my birth control pills. That wasn't good for either of us.

Big Red had a couple of other unpleasant tendencies too. If you left your alcoholic beverage unattended for even a moment, he'd finish it. I've seen that dog inebriated more times than a former child star. Big Red also had the nasty habit of humping almost every male visitor who walked through our door. He also delighted in humping my former mother-in-law's ottoman. He's a kinky beast.

Red is naturally the smartest of all the dogs I've ever had. He can break into any place and any thing, and I'm pretty sure he could crack open a safe if the need arose. Yet the quintessential Big Red story to date happened in the summer of 2001.

My ex-husband Jon and I were walking the five mutts in a dog-friendly park, when all of a sudden Big Red bolted from the herd. He had spotted a family enjoying a quiet picnic on the other side of the ravine, and before we could catch up to him, Big Red had jumped up on their picnic table. He gulped down all their peanut butter sandwiches, terrorized their tiny lapdog by chasing it around the table several times, and then closed the show by relieving himself on their hibachi (thereby extinguishing the flames). The family was a combination of furious and horrified, and began screaming at us in another language. Unfortunately, Jon and I were both doubled over in hysterics, which only further angered the innocent picnickers.

Like any charming bad boy, Big Red always gets away with these shenanigans because he's a very affectionate and emotional dog. He has this adorable habit of napping in empty bath tubs, and he will lick your face until you are completely devoid of makeup. Did I mention that he has the softest fur ever, and that his tummy always smells like Sun Chips?

Big Red is older now and not quite as mischievous, yet he still has that certain glimmer in his eyes which makes me believe that if I ever walked in on him unexpectedly, I would catch him with a hooker.

Kickin' it old school

"The things which the child loves remain in the domain of the heart until old age."
—KAHLIL GIBRAN

Did you ever notice that when you reminisce about events in your childhood and recall certain acquaintances from back in the day, you always refer to them by both their first and last names? If I'm talking about the neighborhood where I grew up, public school or dance class, I invariably recollect my childhood buddies' full names: Sara Ricciotti, Linda Listenchuk, Marnie Sutherland, Eddy Freeburn, Monique Dugas, Sheila Lauzon, Tara McGee, etc. I swear to you, I could easily list another fifty names from my past, yet I can't even remember the first name of someone I met at a function last night.

It's wild how our childhood friends tattoo us so deeply. These early relationships are very intimate in so many ways. Recently, someone from my past e-mailed me. I won't possibly cop to how many years it's been since we last laid eyes on each other, but suffice it to say that we were aged seven and nine respectively (I was the older woman).

Steven Manchulenko, as he so eloquently pointed out in his ubersweet e-mail to me, lived a couple of houses down from us in Sault Ste. Marie. Bobby Dumanski lived next to Steven, and adjacent to Bobby were our wonderful next door neighbors: the McMillans. As Steven reminded me, the McMillans had a big black dog called Mr. Jiggs.

One summer when there was a drought, and therefore little in the way of berries or vegetation for the wildlife to eat, several bears made their way into the city. Our house was almost completely surrounded by woods, and a couple of Mama Bears had appeared in our backyard rifling through garbage cans in the hope of finding some vegan treats for their youngsters. One had also taken a stroll through the front lobby of the Holiday Inn and had become stuck between the sliding doors. She was eventually tranquilized and safely transported back to her natural habitat… a Best Western.

One evening I was coming home from a friend's place in the 'hood, and I saw Mr. Jiggs at the bottom of our driveway. I hit the brakes, popped off my bike, and started to pet my favorite doggie. The big furry thing was facing away from me, and the moment I touched the animal it swung around with a faint growl. All my parents heard was, "YOU'RE NOT MR. JIGGS!!!" and I ran so fast away from the bear cub that I practically left the silhouette of my body on the closed screen door.

Steven reminisced about how he and my younger brother would build forts in our backyard and trade G.I. Joe paraphernalia. He remembered that my parents had a blue Ford, and recalled how he and my little brother often fought over which one of them was going to marry me. How hilarious is that? Keep in mind, my brother would have been three or four.

Steven also wrote to inquire about my brother. Apparently, the day Stephen moved from our cozy subdivision to Sudbury, Ontario, my brother had given him a tiny picture of himself. Stephen has always kept that old picture in an album. Then Steven wrote this: "The clearest memory I have of you was when I saw you walking up the street toward my house. I grabbed a hammer or something and dove under my mom's car to make you think I was working on it. I wanted to impress you since I had such a crush on you and I had to win you away from your brother. You said to me, 'Working on your car, eh?' I was quite happy to see that you noticed."

After reading these words my heart had a meltdown. Not only did this transport me back in time, but it shone a new light and perspective on that particular *époque*. I had always thought that Steven Manchulenko loathed me. I was such a gangly geek that I had naturally assumed I was just the annoying older sister who would intrude upon his time with his buddy. My clearest memory of Steven was the time we were play-fighting and he smashed a Tonka truck on the top of my coconut. In light of this new information from him, I can now confirm unequivocally, that when a boy *likes you,* he shows it by punching you in the arm or pulling on your ponytail. And when he *really likes you,* he pretty much needs to hit you over the head to get your attention.

CHAPTER 4

Angels Travel in Rack Packs

"There is a special place in hell for women who do not help other women."
—MADELEINE K. ALBRIGHT

Initially, I was going to call this fourth and final category of angels "Girl-on-Girl Action" in order to get everyone's attention. I know every man's fantasy is to watch two women together. Sadly, this fantasy doesn't work in reverse. No woman ever wants to see two men together. You never hear anyone say, "Hey, Penn and Teller, I just wish they were naked and tickling each other."

Unlike in porn, women don't always play so well together. Although this is a generalization, women often hate on each other. I guess because my mother was such a great role model and friend I've never subscribed to this. Nor have I fully understood why men have such a strong brotherhood and team-player mentality while women tend to tear each other apart.

I have always had amazing girlfriend mojo. I am blessed to be surrounded by the most extraordinary and wonderful angel-women imaginable. Not unlike my imaginary friends, my female buddies come from all walks of life; have varying ages, beliefs, vocations, sexual orientations, nationalities and backgrounds. Some are married, some are single, some are mothers, some are not; and some are absolutely certifiable... in a good way. Some have been my friends forever, and some are fabulous new kindred spirits.

Stepher and I have been best friends since we were sixteen. The only way to describe her is with the adjective *magical*. Stephanie still has the ability to make me heartsick when she leaves after a visit. She's now a high school principal who kayaks to work in the Queen Charlotte Islands.

My friend Lana is a single mother of five who makes raising children (*sans* nanny or housekeeper) always seem effortless; and she's been making me laugh and supporting my dreams since we were teens.

I have lovingly watched my friend Catherine battle and conquer breast cancer with unbelievable grace and strength. I also witnessed my friend Marcy, with her unstinting positive attitude and phenomenal sense of humor, undergo countless radiation treatments for a brain tumor.

Christine and Penelope are the big sisters I never had. I greatly admire them both, and their success and generosity never cease to amaze me. Donna is a southern belle who taught me to save the environment and introduced me to the merits of Wild Turkey.

I would never have survived university if it hadn't been for my beautiful and brilliant roommate Heather. For years, my dear friend Vivian has doubled as my therapist and spiritual advisor. My amazing friend Sandy, who after meeting me one night at a mutual friends' birthday party, opened up her home to me. I ended up staying with Sandy and her family my entire first year in L.A. Finally, my wonderful new friend Stacy has become a godmother to our dogs and now works as my social media publicist. Stacy's techno-savvy has helped me immensely because when it comes to computers, I'm just a bonnet away from being Amish.

There are so many more remarkable women I want to introduce that it could fill an entire book. These ladies are all angels to me; and they are all absolutely gorgeous, which makes me either incredibly secure or stupid—and I think we all know I'm less secure than the Mexican border.

My point is that women should rally together in support of each other. Catfights are so 1982, and I'm still bewildered as to why or how we can still be our own worst enemy.

Men bond easily and forgive quickly. At 1 a.m., two dudes can almost stab each other during a heated *contretemps* at a Mexican cockfight. By 2 a.m. they will be laughing together over a few tequila shots.

Men have formed such a brotherhood that it has recently even produced a new film subgenre called "bromance" movies. These are essentially movies where the plot is driven by the special friendship between the two male leads. I don't think these buddy flicks qualify as bromances. The only bromance I can think of is *Brokeback Mountain*. Seriously dudes, just because you put a masculine prefix in front of some very metrosexual behavior doesn't necessarily man it up: "Hey Mark, wanna come over tonight and do some *manscaping* together? I know you're having *manstrual* cramps but I'll give you a 'guydol' and you'll be good to go."

Look what's happening, ladies. We need to form an alliance together as tightly knit as the men's. We have to do something about this. Men already dominate action flicks, Westerns and war movies. Now they are taking romantic comedies away from us. Women have become redundant in these bromance films. If this keeps up, what do you think will happen to Kate Hudson and Cameron Diaz? For the love of shoes!

Women have to drop the petty jealousies, insecurities and judgments so that we can band together and form fabulous relationships with one another. It's ridiculous to not get along with each other when we are all basically the same person. So when we get together, we'll have lots to talk about.

All women are slightly crazy. That's why we're so much fun. Maybe not Lindsay- or Courtney-crazy, but we're all definitely in the Macy Gray area. All women have deep-tongued their best friend after one too many shots of tequila. All women snoop. Every woman on earth has read a co-worker's e-mails, rummaged through her dude's apartment, or been party to a stake-out. I don't know what it is about us, but we must all suffer from private dick envy.

And finally, all women, at some point in their lives have faked an orgasm. Next time might I suggest faking *not* having an orgasm? It requires some discipline, but it keeps junior down there a lot longer.

I believe I have successfully proven my point foxy ladies. Now let's unite in the spirit of sisterhood and celebrate our feminine mystique. Once we do this, we'll take over this mother-lovin' planet.

Heroines instead of heroin

"When you're going through hell... keep going."
—LAURA HART

In 2005, my life fell apart like the back end of *Saturday Night Live*. Every corner of my world came crashing down. The unraveling of my family was the most painful because it had always been what I had cherished the most in this world.

According to the Kabbalists, you don't wake up one day and notice a giant oak tree in your backyard. I am grateful to my dad for being a good father during my formative years, but the truth of the matter is that he had been going south for a very long time. It would appear that he had been leading a double life for years. Everything came to a head in an eighteen-month period of time that saw me posting bail for his release from a Florida prison, to discovering that he had a severe gambling addiction.

My dad's downward spiral and erratic behavior devastated my mother. He was the love of her life and they had been together since she was a teenager. His emotional bankruptcy resulted in the rest of the family's near-actual bankruptcy, and took an enormous toll on my brother and me. We survived and bonded through a lot of dark humor and some much-needed open communication.

It's a double-edged sword to be very close with your family when heavy trauma and drama occur. There's absolutely no way to distance yourselves from one another. I felt my family's pain with every fiber of my being; just as I'm sure my mother and brother felt mine. My father had been my childhood hero, and would now become the only man to ever break my heart into a million pieces. After years of pretending that everything was fine, and never admitting to the slightest crack in my family's plaster, I was now being crushed under the weight of all the skeletons in my closet.

On top of my family life turning into a bad movie of the week, 2005 and early 2006 ushered in the end of my first marriage during a time when I had absolutely no career to speak of in order to distract me from the hot mess of my personal life. To compound things further, I also had no fixed address for several months, my car was stolen from a parking lot in L.A., and that Christmas, the airline lost my luggage (which contained almost my entire wardrobe). The added insults? My face broke out so badly that I needed to wear a burka before leaving the house, and I developed a fibroid cyst in my tummy the size of a cantaloupe. Good times!

As Michael J. Fox once said, "We all have our bag of hammers." I recognize that many people have been through far worse ordeals than the ones I was grappling with, but it was a pretty low, dark period for me. I was clearly lost in hell, and refused to stop and ask for directions. Outside of my immediate family, I told almost no one of my trials and tribulations. I should have won an Emmy.

Fortunately, my new friend and angel, Bunny, had recently entered my life. Bunny is a feisty, crazy, beautiful woman who delivers every filthy nugget out of her mouth with the authority and confidence of a CEO. Not surprising considering she has a masters degree in business and a PhD in moxie. Bunny has bigger balls than an NBA player and swears like a member of the Soprano family. She is a no-nonsense, solutions-oriented hustler who could sell suicide bombs to the Taliban. She also has a penchant for delivering unorthodox yet valuable advice on an hourly basis. Ironically, Bunny is the size of an action figure with more energy than a toddler hopped up on a case of Red Bull. She is a mother who claims to loathe most children, and confesses she has only recently taken a liking to her own two sons. This one-time party girl, who could out-drink David Hasselhoff, didn't exactly sport wings and a halo. She did, however, possess some other superpowers, like the uncanny ability to divine what I was going through. Bunny was able to empathize with my nasty situation, and obviously recognized some of the signs. This is due largely to the fact that she has a heart the size of Manhattan, and because she spends most of her time focused on and caring for others.

Not only was Bunny my confidante throughout all the madness, but she also showed me an unparalleled generosity that overwhelms me to this day (and for which I will never adequately be able to thank her).

The morning my ex-husband and I decided to split, I was obviously very distraught. Naturally, Bunny phoned just when I needed her most and convinced me to stop sobbing and haul my ass out to the best restaurant in the city so she could buy me lunch and numb my hurt with copious amounts of champagne. She pulled up to the eatery in an SUV filled with clothing and shoes to replace my missing wardrobe (don't ask me how we're the same size!).

Throughout the year she managed to get me gigs so that I could pay the bills, and when I debuted with my one-woman show in Toronto, she strong-armed all of her wealthy friends into purchasing entire nights of the production so that the show would sell out. I could cite countless other incredible acts of kindness she exhibited throughout the worst time of my life. In addition, during this rather challenging phase for my family, Bunny was also an amazing friend to my mother and my brother.

There are times now when I'm walking on the beach or working on a show and my mind will drift back to those difficult months. My eyes inevitably well up with tears of gratitude over everything that woman did for me. I will never forget it. She is my closest friend to this day. She is one in a billion, and certainly an angel who most definitely saved my life.

Talk about opening up the third eye

"When all is shit, become a fly."
—JOSH HOLMAN

The other angel who miraculously (albeit ironically) appeared when my life was in the crapper was Eloise, the psychic colon therapist. That's right; although I'm sure she hates the fact that I bill her as such. Eloise is indeed a colon therapist, nutritionist and homeopathic healer whom I frequent on a regular basis. She also happens to be extremely and eerily intuitive. Sure, sometimes I wish she would just read my tea leaves, but I do enjoy the fact that she is getting rid of poo from 1985.

To be honest, there are times when I'm not entirely certain Eloise is actually a citizen of this planet. She has an astonishing ability to read people and call them on their shit (pardon the pun) within seconds of meeting them. If she isn't an astral goddess, then she's as close to divine as you can get without actually seeing a white light and deceased family members. I think she is unbelievably evolved and gifted.

I recently asked Eloise, "Why colon therapy?" I mean, I thought dentists had it rough spending their entire day looking into someone's orifice. She revealed to me that she had been stricken with polio as a child. This is a pretty old-school and devastating disease, and Eloise's mother treated her using a variety of homeopathic remedies, including colonics twice a week. Eloise isn't sure exactly how it all worked, but she was cured and never suffered any side effects.

Eloise grew up to become an accomplished concert pianist and avid surfer who worked for years as a studio musician. When her mother, a cancer survivor, suffered a massive heart attack and was only given six months to live, Eloise decided it was now her turn to be the caregiver. So she left the music biz in order to treat her mother using a combination of Chinese herbs, homeopathic medicines and colon therapy. Her mother lived ten years longer than the doctor's original prediction. Eloise continues to improve and save lives on a daily basis. There are thousands of people she has healed over the years, and I'm one of them.

Eloise has taught me the importance of forgiving and letting go. She is still trying to get me to develop more patience than a two-year-old, and also urges me to get out of my own way. This apparently means to calm down, stop judging myself harshly, and to stop beating the crap out of myself. She'll take care of that in a kinder, gentler way.

According to Eloise, she subscribes to colon therapy because it keeps the nervous and lymph systems active as well as keeping the muscles active. Colonics keep the body running well and clear out all the gunk from our emotional bodies. Amen. I bet my "emotional body" was like a New York sewer.

Eloise is all about teaching the true art of joyful living. She evoked the popular number three when she threw down: "Life, consciousness and bliss." I countered that this all sounded delightful, but how the hell do we plebeians get there? I mean, when someone suffers a major loss, is dealing with a life-threatening disease, or simply finds themselves in the depths of despair, telling them to "think positively" may result in you getting cold-cocked in the face, non?

Here's the advice Eloise shared: "When something horrific or traumatic happens, the key is to just keep breathing. Breathing is the power source of life and what separates us from everyone at Forest Lawn Cemetery. Just breathe and take stock of your life. Then you need to start to move out of the problem and towards the solution. Don't get comfy and take up residence in the problem. Look for the lesson, the light and the solution. Don't see yourself knee-deep in shit but standing in a pile of fertilizer... it's got a better spin to it."

She added, "Plus, whatever happened is now already in the past. Why worry about the past? People make the mistake of basing their present state on where they have been instead of who they are now. Live in the absolute present."

She advises that we shouldn't stay engaged in negative thought or behavior, but we should step out and attempt to see our life objectively. That way we can watch and identify unhealthy, reoccurring patterns in order to avoid a big hit. Exercise, a good diet full of fruits and vegetables (some I had literally never heard of), and meditation were all essential in order to achieve inner joy. Eloise believes that refined sugars keep our systems agitated and inflated, and should be avoided at all costs. Basically, refined sugars are pure evil.

Eloise is convinced that as individuals, and as a society, we must stop blaming others and hating on them. We need to take full responsibility for ourselves and move to a point of self-realization. She strongly suggested that we should "allow people to be people and accept their differences."

When I mentioned that fear seemed to be man's greatest enemy, she offered how fear could be man's greatest motivator. Her advice is, "Just do right by the planet... start local and spread out."

Eloise closed by saying that we need to use the power of our minds more. She claims the average person uses only 2 percent of their brain; Einstein used 16 percent. I asked, "How do we tap into more of our brain?" She answered, "Meditate and don't stay in the shallow. You can't flit around all the time; butterflies have short lives. Think about something other than sex." There you have it: sage advice from a true master.

I love Eloise. She's an angel—an angel who gives me colonics.

CARE AND TREATMENT OF YOUR

Angels

) Make sure to water your angels at least twice a week.

) Angels are machine washable, but must be put on the delicate cycle.

) Always be grateful for and to your angels.

) Don't put too much pressure on your angels; they don't want you to become co-dependent.

) Angels love it when you laugh and/or dance as it is physically impossible to be in a pissy mood while doing either.

) Get more in touch with your spiritual side. For example, try reading *The Secret*... while pleasuring yourself.

) Angels should be walked or taken outside on a daily basis. They also love it when you are on the move. Stay busy.

) Meditate. Angels have a difficult time talking to you if there's a lot of noise such as annoying techno music playing in the soundtrack of your life.

) Don't get too clingy with your angels; it turns them off.

) Don't take yourself too seriously; your angels sure as hell don't.

) Give your angels the majority of your energy instead of focusing on the assholes in your life. The bad kid getting all your time and attention is so five minutes ago.

) Angels like it when you have pets in your home because they move the energy around and it's good feng shui.

) Angels encourage you to visualize whatever it is you

want from life. This may include anything from picturing yourself healthy and happy and working at your new dream job, to picturing Robert Downey, Jr. and Gerard Butler taking turns sponge bathing you.

❱ Don't expect an exact exchange. Perhaps there is someone in your life like a spouse, a family member or a friend to whom you give everything. Maybe you are constantly offering complete emotional and financial support. If this person gives you little in return (and if you are not being an enabler), relax. You must give unconditionally and without expecting anything. You are probably the angel in this scenario. Trust me, you will get back everything you give and much more from others in your world. It's just not a direct exchange of energy. I'm sure you can think of someone or several people who have probably given much more to you in your life than you were ever able to repay.

❱ Angels enjoy it when you pipe up and genuinely compliment friends or strangers. This can often make someone's day. Angels appreciate the Kanye West lyrics: "When you admire someone tell'em. People only send flowers when you can't smell'em." That's right, angels are fans of Kanye's music.

❱ Do not build a Berlin Wall around you to stay protected. Sure it will keep the douche bags out, but it will also prevent you from letting the angels in.

❱ Stay true to your own belief system and integrity. Whether you believe in God, the Universe, the light source, Bono, or just being kind to everyone; go with what resonates for you. Just remember to give others the freedom without judgment to follow their own paths and beliefs. Angels are faith-blind.

PART II

Vampires

vam·pire [**vam**-p*ahyuh*r]
—noun

1. a preternatural being, commonly believed to be a reanimated corpse, which is said to suck the blood of sleeping persons at night.

2. a person who preys ruthlessly upon others; extortionist.

"Count Dracula may not seem like the ideal husband. Of course, he's deathly pale, but he's a vegetarian, and they all seem to look like that."
—MAXIME MCKENDRY, ANDY WARHOL'S DRACULA

My definition of a vampire casts a wider net and includes all people and things that are seductive, sexy and trendy, but ultimately may not be truly beneficial to us and sometimes may even kill us. Vampires may seem irresistible, but remember, they are parasites who live off your blood, drain your energy, and can steal your soul. A vampire is also anyone or anything that takes your power away from you. Sure, vampires are alluring and fashionable, but they are also dangerous. Remember, even the lovable Count Floyd, as portrayed by Joe Flaherty on *SCTV*, was a chain-smoking gambler.

Can someone tell me why vampires are so hot? They're pale, effeminate, and they always seem like they're in a bitchy mood. They look like confused Euro-transgenders dressed like Johnny Cash. I just don't understand why the undead are the new black. I thought Tom Cruise officially killed the genre with his portrayal of Anne Rice's Lestat. But vampires are more popular than ever. There are countless television shows and movies celebrating all that is fanged.

Apparently, vampires are irresistible to women. Frank Langella has a theory: "Vampires are sexy to women, perhaps because the fantasy is similar to that of the man on the white horse sweeping them off to paradise." Personally, I don't think for a nanosecond that a relationship with a vampire is going to lead to a happy ending in Shangri-La. I think it's only going to result in a bad hickey and sun deprivation. Yet everyone's in love with that dude from the

Twilight series, and the boys from *True Blood* are megahot! Hell, right now even Count von Count from *Sesame Street* is probably tapping a MILF. Honestly, what's the attraction? It's like having a crush on the goth guy in high school who always got the shit kicked out of him. Rob Pattinson, star of the *Twilight* movies, wears more eyeliner than the lead singer of The Cure. I guess I can't judge him too harshly; it's not like he can check his makeup in the mirror!

I'm baffled. Why are vampires the heartthrobs of the ghoul kingdom? Why do ladies love vampires? And trust me, they do. How else do you think Keith Richards still gets laid? Why not go for mummies? They're rich, they're royalty, and they want to beat the crap out of Brendan Fraser—so the two of you already have something in common. And why isn't Frankenstein more alluring? He's the strong silent type, he's a good Jewish boy, he's mentored by a doctor, and if he's built to proportion—then he's hung... well, like a monster.

Vampires don't just morph into bats. They are shape-shifters who take on a myriad of forms on earth. They aren't classic mythical beings but wily creatures that attract us, tempt us, and eventually suck all the life out of us.

It's time to shed some much-needed light on these beguiling vampires by pulling back their long capes and exposing them for the predators and leeches they are. I can't solve all the vampire mysteries though. I'll never understand how George Hamilton, with his permanent man tan, was cast as a vampire in the movie *Love at First Bite*.

Chapter 5

Bad Boys and Crazy Bitches

"Women might be able to fake orgasms.
But men fake entire relationships."

—SHARON STONE

This first category of vampires is perhaps the best known and most enchanting. Easily the most attractive of the vampire species, the timeless appeal of the bad boy cannot be denied—especially when the woman's age starts with a *two*.

Men have always divided women into two categories: wholesome or sexy. They either fall for Betty or Veronica, Mary-Ann or Ginger, Jennifer Aniston or Angelina Jolie. Basically, they are faced with the dilemma of choosing between the nice girl next door they can bring home to mom, or the often promiscuous, slightly dangerous girl who will scream, "Who's your mommy?" We're talking the quintessential Madonna–whore complex, which may possibly date back to the Virgin Mary and Mary Magdalene.

Well, this can be applied to guys as well. Two archetypal men appear throughout history, literature and pop culture: The stable and reliable do-gooder who dotes on his lady—versus the elusive, impenetrable, uber-masculine, smokin'-hot bad boy who always remains just a little out of reach and writes his own rules.

In *Casablanca*, the stable and upstanding community organizer, Victor Laszlo, is pitted against the renegade, hard-drinking casino manager Rick. In *Star Wars,* the choice is between the fresh-faced greenhorn Jedi Knight Luke Skywalker, who spent a great deal of time pining for his sister—and Han Solo, the brutally handsome wise-cracking loner who piloted the Millennium Falcon (with the help of a Wookie) and answered, "I know" when Princess Leia declared her love for him. More recently, *Sex and the City* nice guy and dog-loving nature boy Aidan, finished last to Mr. Big's wealthy, commitment-impaired playboy. In each of the above scenarios, the woman opts for the sexy bad boy. The only reason Ingrid Bergman stayed with Laszlo was because Bogie forced her to for the good of the cause. I wish the good, devoted and trustworthy men who offered security and unconditional love in these stories had been painted with a few more desirable strokes.

Since it is our innate desire to seek out that which we cannot completely possess or control, I blame pop culture for making the bad boy the far more enticing character to fall for. Resistance is futile now that we have to deal with the quintessential seductive bad boy Don Draper, the mysterious advertising genius in *Mad Men*. This ridiculously handsome, tall, dark, incorrigible womanizer who smokes and drinks constantly, is so emotionally unavailable that he is more likely to access the Internet in 1963 than his own feelings. Yet every woman I know wants to jump his inaccessible bones with the enthusiasm of a horny cheerleader.

We have to keep in mind that the fictional bad boy, like the fictional vampire, is far more appealing than the real-life creature. Sure, sometimes bad boys are immature and eventually grow into responsible men, but I've witnessed many women lose the best years of their lives waiting around for their philandering rebels to rehabilitate and become loyal, loving partners. As sexy as these aloof Romeos may seem, do you really want them to be the father of your children? If you're truly seeking someone you can't communicate with and can never reach, never depend on and rarely get any affection from, why don't you get a cat? A fling with a mysterious stranger is fine, but if he's still a stranger ten years down the road it gets a little tired. And for the love of Thor, do not get involved with a married man. I don't care if you can cite the one shining example of your janitor's sister's niece whose affair with a married man evolved into a happily-ever-after tale. Hear this: He is NEVER going to leave his wife for you. You are wasting your life and will remain the other woman until you die and become the otherworldly woman. Besides, it's just crappy karma.

If your bad boy is an adult, then he may be a bad man. Women always think they can reform these players and mold them into the kind, loyal providers and respectable, faithful lovers necessary for a long-lasting committed relationship. If you're looking for a fixer-upper, then you're better off purchasing an old duplex.

The bottom line is—not all sexy bad boys are vampires. Some are fairly harmless and can be good times. If you're not looking for anything serious, enjoy the Don Juans and see what develops (as long as what develops isn't Chlamydia!). Just use a safe... and a safe word... and you should be fine. If your bad boy becomes a full-on vampire, ask yourself whether someone who stays out all night, sleeps all day, and turns into a nasty rodent when he's angry is your idea of the perfect dream man or a recurring nightmare?

"By the time I found out just how crazy she was, it was too late.
I was forced to sleep over. I spent the entire night lying next to her with
one eye open like a Mexican cat."
—RICK COLLINS

If we're talking female vampires, crazy is definitely the new hot. Women crush on bad boys; and who's the companion weakness for men? Crazy bitches. It seems that men are undeniably attracted to women who are completely certifiable. From time immemorial, men have been drawn to bitches—the type of woman who treats them like crap and never takes any from them.

When you add crazy to the mix, it's an unbeatable cocktease cocktail that no mortal man can resist. I'm not entirely sure why, but I believe it's because men equate crazy with good in bed. Men figure that the kookier some broad acts, the more likely she is to throw down some type of Cirque du Soleil maneuvers in the boudoir that they've never seen before. If a man spots a woman wandering aimlessly down the street dressed like an American Civil War re-enactor, sniffing her own armpits and clucking like a chicken—and if that woman is even remotely hot—trust me, the guy is thinking she gives wicked blow jobs.

Many female celebrities are perpetuating this idea. Every young thing in Hollywood insists on exiting limos commando-style, starlets are in and out of rehab like food through a bulimic, and Lindsay Lohan has crashed more often than my hard drive. The crazier a woman acts, the more attention and press she gets. That's why many actresses act nuttier than squirrel shit!

Men love crazy bitches because men hate routine

and predictability. Having a girlfriend with a multiple personality disorder makes a guy feel like he's not in a monogamous relationship. In addition, a crazy bitch is also liable to be a tad dangerous, thus combining two of men's favorite genres: porn and action flicks. Men love to get close to the fire, that's why they are fond of barbecuing. Unfortunately, these particular dudes are far more likely to get burned.

I know you guys think that having a wild woman who is capable of anything is a turn-on, but how will you feel a week into the relationship when she's sporting a tattoo of your junk on her left shoulder and carrying around a zip lock bag full of your shorn chest hairs in her purse? And are you still going to think your crazy bitch is hot when she shows up to your office buck naked, keys your car, sleeps with your father, and insists on making tea using nothing but hot water and your boxer shorts? If you're into that kind of thing, have a go at it. If not, think carefully before you get involved with a psycho she-devil who will make your life hell. I know this type of female vampire is tempting, but remember—they're immortal; and if you're not looking to turn your tryst with a crazy bitch into a long-term relationship, how are you going to handle eternity with this berserk broad? She'll suck and swallow the life out of you.

My first Dracula

*"France has neither winter nor summer nor morals.
Apart from these drawbacks it is a fine country."*
—MARK TWAIN

I spent my third year of university in Besançon, France as part of an exchange program between the University of Western Ontario and the Université de Franche Comté. Besançon is a small medieval town a few hours southeast of Paris by train. The school had no dormitory to speak of, so I agreed to rent a tiny room in the city, sight unseen, before I traveled over the pond. To my surprise and sheer delight, I found myself staying in a modern-day castle because the owner of the home was an architect. I literally had to climb up the stairs of a tower to reach my quaint little bedroom. My French family was absolutely wonderful. Their eldest daughter had recently left the nest and I swashbuckled in nicely as a surrogate child.

In Besançon, I immersed myself in the French language and its culture and history, and most weekends I traveled to nearby countries: Italy, Switzerland, Germany and Spain. Although the actual college was a bit of a disappointment (one of my professors was always completely wasted and was convinced that he was the reincarnation of famed French author Victor Hugo) I had one of the most magical years of my life.

I often broke bread with my new French family, and I became completely fluent in the language. I even began working at a local radio station. My show was called *Les Heures Chaudes avec Carla* (The Hot Hours with Carla), and no other DJ was able to pronounce my Anglophone name.

The owner of the station was an older man called Philippe LeGrand (Phillip the Great) who looked like the love child of Warren Beatty and Roman Polanski (which may be entirely possible). He was a dark, dashing, handsome thirty-seven-year-old whom I found terribly erudite and worldly. He was also a local celebrity prone to wandering the city wearing a cape and knee-high leather boots. He struck me as rather exotic and intriguing. Philippe spent months pursuing me by constantly whispering "*Je vous aime*" in my ear. By the way, *Je vous aime* translates roughly into "I love thee," which I found unusual yet charming.

When I began dating Philippe, my French family was thrilled that their roomer had landed such a high-profile catch. I was twenty-one and still a virgin (if Bill Clinton rules apply). Part of my romantic master plan was to make love in the rolling hills of the majestic French countryside. So one night when I was drunk on red wine and my strange new surroundings, Philippe seduced me in his turn-of-the-century mansion (which he shared with his sixteen-year-old daughter and seventeen-year-old son— awkward!). Our torrid (and slightly forbidden) affair lasted throughout the summer and long after the other Canadians, who were part of the same exchange, returned back home. I was determined to stay in France with my new lover and his teenaged children. My parents were horrified, and they finally convinced me to come back to Canada just days before my fourth year of university was to begin.

My re-entry into London, Ontario was a difficult one. Upon my return I chain-smoked, quoted Voltaire incessantly, and complained that Canada was a country in its infancy. I finally recovered from my French hangover malaise when my mother informed me that I was to stop acting like an asshole or she would disown me. I got back into my studies with a vengeance (considering I had failed a course in France and was carrying an extra subject) and slipped into the rhythm of living at Saugeen-Maitland Hall, where I worked as a don in charge of three floors.

It was at this time that Philippe decided to make an unannounced visit to my residence at Western. What was romantic and eccentric in France definitely got lost in translation in my preppy university surroundings. Philippe did not speak a word of English, and when he dramatically entered the campus bars wearing his trademark cape and knee-high boots, with his jet black hair slicked back, he no longer looked liked a movie star. He looked like an aging, gay Count Chocula. This did not end well. In fact, it ended with me gently explaining to Philippe that our long-distance relationship would not work out, and with Philippe yelling French obscenities at me in my dorm room as he was hurling thick, French textbooks at my head. So you see, I too fell for a vampire who ended up biting me in the ass.

Milan is beautiful this time of year

"Perfection is finally attained not when there is no longer anything to add but when there is no longer anything to take away, when a body has been stripped down to its nakedness."
—ANTOINE DE SAINT-EXUPÉRY

Very early on in my relationship with my husband Ty, the two of us went to a party in Hollywood. We were at some trendy restaurant on the Sunset Strip and there was a whole lot of lameness going on. Horrible techno music pounded away while several hundred strangers posed with drinks that cost more than iPhones. It just wasn't our scene. So Ty and I were in and out of there like Navy SEALs, and en route back to our car we passed a strip joint. I had never been to a "gentlemen's club" in my life, and thought it might be something sexy and adventurous for us to do together (besides, we had already dropped $20 on parking). Although Ty seemed a tad shocked when his nice, new Canadian girlfriend suggested a peek inside a peeler palace, he still lit up like a Christmas tree.

Here's the thing: I had no idea that they don't serve alcohol in all-nude strip clubs in California. When the waitress came over to our table and offered us Perrier or Red Bull, I assumed she said it was because there was a "full moon." What? It's L.A. Goofier things have happened. She corrected me and said "full nude," and I proceeded to giggle nervously. I don't know about you, but I need beer with my nipples, especially when I took a gander around at that sad, dark cave with poles. This place smelled like vanilla body spray and desperation. Every woman on stage was heavily made-up and bejeweled, and the guys in the audience looked like creepy, slumped-over trolls. It was like the Persian orgy scene from the movie *300;* not at all what I had imagined.

Suddenly, a tiny, nubile young thing dressed in a bikini and thigh-high moccasin boots came strutting over. She looked like a slutty Pocahontas. She encouraged us to get a couples' lap dance because it would be "sensual and lead to tantric sex." I hesitated, because to me, tantric sex sounds a lot like a Kevin Costner movie—it goes on forever and nobody comes. Nevertheless, we followed this little pixie past the ATM machines through to the even darker backroom where she set up two collapsible chairs side by side. Ty and I gingerly took our places on the adjacent seats, and I took a deep breath. Our dancer introduced herself as "Milan" (natch) and began to limber up by putting her left leg around the back of her neck. She also began chatting us up like a Vegas performer warming up the crowd at The Palms. She must have asked me a dozen questions and complimented me on both my haircut and choice of outfit. While I was impressed with her flexibility, I wasn't expecting to make small talk with a stripper.

As I sat there in pure abject fear, shaking like a Chihuahua hopped up on double espressos and Jagermeister, I was thinking, "Why is it talking? No, it rubs the lotion on its skin." Mercifully, the next song started (that's what Milan had been waiting for) and she immediately stopped talking and straddled my man. Before I knew it, she was on Ty's package like R. Kelly on a babysitter. I didn't know whether I was aroused or whether I wanted to clock the little minx. After what seemed like hours, she turned her attention to me and began grinding on my breasts with the intensity of a thousand burning suns. Now granted, I call my breasts "Tom and Katie" because they're not for real either, but that doesn't give a stranger license to knead them like stale pizza dough. The irony is, I'm not sure if Ty had even touched my breasts at this point. I just know that throughout the entire process I remained perfectly still like a wild forest animal that doesn't want to be spotted by its prey.

At the end of the song, Ty's shirt was off, Milan was completely naked, and I was certain I was pregnant. She suggested another song but I knew that these dances escalated, and I thought to myself, "What the hell happens next?" Fearing this would turn into *Caligula* or something illegal in most States, we simply thanked her, gathered ourselves and walked back to the car in silence.

I must admit, later that night we consummated our relationship with the most incredible, passionate jungle sex imaginable. So if your relationship needs a little boost, might I suggest a trip to Milan?

Chapter 6

Beware of False Prophets and Fake Breasts

"I'm not a prophet or a stone aged man, just a mortal with potential of a superman. I'm living on."

—DAVID BOWIE

This next sect of vampires consists of the blood suckers who prey upon others, as well as the baby vampires—superficial, material toys that can sometimes distract us from what truly matters.

In the interest of full disclosure, I must cop to the fact that for years now I have left no mystical stone unturned. Every conceivable New Age, self-help, quasi-religious or deeply superstitious practice was fair game. My exhaustive search for universal truths was so extensive that it would leave a Tibetan monk speechless. Oh wait, they already are....

I admit that I consult with no fewer than six to eight psychics on a regular basis, just to reference and cross-check. But psychics are for entertainment purposes only and are not a very good investment, considering most of them have the accuracy of a MapQuest estimated time. Although some soothsayers I have frequented had terribly enlightening insights, I am troubled by one nagging thought—psychics are the only people on the planet who still use cassette tapes. Think about it. Your future is recorded on an obsolete format. If these prognosticators can truly predict what's ahead, shouldn't they have envisioned MP3 players and CDs decades ago?

Fortunately, I am blessed to have a couple of friends who are truly gifted and intuitive. They are healers who vibrate at a higher level, and they never hawk their wares on the street or in a small bungalow with a neon sign that glows: "PSYCHIC READINGS." Many so-called psychics appear to be less stable than the economy, and they often look like a cross between a homeless Norma Desmond and a post-rehab Amy Winehouse. These aren't psychics; they're idiot-clair-voyants. When you think about it, you're putting your hopes and dreams into the hands of someone you wouldn't trust to water your plants while you're on vacation.

I must also admit that the rack I'm sporting is not my own. That's right; they're fake and they're spectacular. But I do wish I had the option of taking them on and off like Lee Press-On Knobs. What can I tell you? Dr. Bill did an awesome job and my husband loves them, but it was an impulse buy. I was at the counter and figured I needed a pack of Mentos, a copy of People magazine, and a bag of boobies. Sure I liked them when I first got them, and they had that new breast smell. I can remember the first time I held one and watched it sleep through the night. It looked just like me. Now they're a couple of years old and they've started to walk. They're getting into everything, it's hard to get a sitter, and I can't turn my back on them.

My mom loves to remind me about how I said I would NEVER get fake breasts. Well, apparently by never I meant a couple of summers ago. I didn't tell mom that I got them done, and I was home for a BBQ a few weeks after Dr. Bill worked his magic. I was eventually busted (as it were) because I was wandering around outside in a big-knitted poncho when it was almost 90°F (and when it wasn't 1974). The thing is, if my new boobs are a bigger issue for you than they are for me, you should check with your mom to see if you were breastfed.

My point is that one should never be too enamored with people who claim to be gurus and try to make you dependent upon them instead of giving you the guidance, confidence and strength to tap into your own light source. Make every attempt to stay away from cult leaders or TV evangelists looking to bilk you out of all your money. These are not masters; they are master manipulators. It's fun to explore different practices and beliefs, but please stop short of entering any establishment where virgins are being sacrificed. I don't have to worry about that kind of thing here in L.A. There are no virgins.

Also, try not to be too distracted by shiny objects. There's absolutely nothing wrong with caring for your physical appearance and desiring material possessions. *Au contraire*, it's healthy. Just make sure it doesn't evolve into the only driving force in your life or you will risk becoming a lemming that is as deep as a lunch tray. Hey, at some point we're all going to look like scrambled eggs, so it might be a good idea to invest in the occasional soul lift.

Oh oh! I'm having a mid-past life crisis

*"You've got as many lives as you like, and more,
even ones you don't want."*

—GEORGE HARRISON

True, I've dabbled in numerology, astrology, healing circles, hypnosis, guided meditation, color therapy, chakra openings, reiki, labyrinths, extreme yoga, and aura readings. I have found most of them infinitely interesting, and for the most part, quite helpful. As you can imagine, I have also run into my share of crazies, especially in L.A. Here, everyone is either a psychic, an actor or a realtor; or a combination of all three. I think my wackiest experience involved Ted, a past-life channeler, and his "gifted" wife who went by the name of Chakra Khan.

The channeler himself looked fairly normal; kind of like an unwashed James Lipton from the *Actors Studio*. However, his wife was more dramatic than an Italian tenor, and appeared to apply her makeup with the subtlety and panache of a drag queen. Chakra looked like an aging magician's assistant with tits 'til Tuesday and a wild blonde mane so out of control that to add any more extensions would have required a zoning permit. She insisted that she had to cleanse my aura before her husband could commence his therapy. She then proceeded to take out what resembled a package of potpourri, and then mixed a dollop of it in a clay bowl with some mystery powder that smelled like feet. As she stirred the magic potion, she chanted what was either an ancient psalm or the lyrics from Pearl Jam's Even Flow. Lighting a match, she set the concoction ablaze in a fiery burst. The stink from the holy herbs engulfed the room in what may well have been the most putrid and heinous odor since the Germans unleashed mustard gas at the Battle of Ypres. I thought for a moment that I might have to pee on my pashmina and hold it over my face just to combat the poisonous stench.

Chakra also offered to give me a "special healing bath" to rinse away and exfoliate all the cells that held on to ugly past memories which no longer served me. I politely passed, and just took an extra-long hot shower when I got home.

The James Lipton-looking guy then instructed me to take a seat closer to him on the couch, then to shut my eyes and breathe normally. He took me through a short guided meditation, and began to count backwards from ten. I assume that it was during this quasi-trance that he performed a past-life regression on me. Like any girl, I fancied my previous incarnations to include poets or princesses—never prostitutes. Yes, the dude with the beard that looked like it was housing a colony of sea monkeys revealed that in my past lives I had been every type of floozy imaginable: harlot, trench whore, slave girl, concubine, gutter slut, etc... with the exception of *one* glorious moment. In one of my past lives, I was a nun who got knocked up by the parish accountant. No wonder I keep coming back.

He also announced that I didn't have an old soul, but that I wasn't a new soul either. Apparently, my soul is middle-aged. Terrific. My soul is sporting a comb-over, driving a Corvette and banging a supermodel.

I still believe in reincarnation though. In my next life, I'm coming back as one of Johnny Depp's tattoos.

The other grandmother

"I could not handle being a woman. I would stay at home all day and play with my breasts."
—STEVE MARTIN

My father's mother was a former beauty queen from Michigan. I must admit that even in her early nineties, Grandma Milly looked better than any of us. Milly was a trip and a half. She sported platinum blonde hair, an unblemished, dewy, creamy complexion, and she was endowed with a giant natural rack that would rival any Baywatch babe. Milly was quite open about the fact that she only cared for good-looking people.

Due to a long unhappy marriage to my Grandpa Jack, Grandma Milly (who lived entirely in the past, and in the superficial) never tired of sharing stories about her stable of former gentlemen callers. As Grandma Milly grew older, she also grew more inappropriate in her storytelling. I remember when she sat my mother and me down and forced us to hear about the night that my father was conceived. No amount of therapy can ever undo the damage from that lovely revelation. It still gives me night sweats. Milly also explained to my brother and me that she was so devastatingly beautiful and irresistible as a young woman that men would (how do I phrase this delicately?) reach orgasm simply by slow dancing with her. I think my brother and I were eleven and sixteen, respectively, when she unleashed that ditty. Oy! Whose grandmother says that? Why couldn't she just crochet doilies and make pies for heaven's sake.

One of my favorite Grandma Milly moments occurred the night of my high school graduation. Let me say that

I adored my high school in Guelph, Ontario, and have nothing but great memories of my years spent there. I met some of my best friends (still to this day) at Guelph Collegiate, and that school was a sanctuary for me during that time. I had been elected valedictorian by my class, so my mom decided that she would throw a party for me and my newly-graduated pals.

Naturally, Grandma Milly insisted on being present for this life moment. She also insisted on wearing her mink coat inside the house throughout the entire party. Grandma held court on the couch the entire evening, causing me to die just a little inside each time she spoke, and causing my mom to hit the white wine often, and hard.

Milly opened by asking all my girlfriends to raise their hands if they were still virgins. No one lifted their arm, so Grandma announced, quite proudly to the entire room, that I still was. I quickly took her aside and gently told her that her line of questioning was highly personal, not to mention embarrassing, and begged her to cease and desist. Alas, this only seemed to spur her on.

Grandma then took it upon herself to inform my boyfriend's younger brother David that I fancied him much more than his elder sibling (which was true, but still...). At that point, I just screamed, "Shut up Grandma Milly!" and tried to create a distraction by spontaneously breaking into dance, even though no music was playing at the time. Undaunted, Grandma just gave me a Cheshire cat grin and retorted with, "Relax dear, I think that gave David a hard-on." There are no words.

Grandma Milly teased me relentlessly about my looks; especially about the fact that I was very flat-chested in contrast to her ample bosom (search no further as to why I eventually had my boobs augmented). In the last decade or so of her life, Grandma Milly even took to flashing me her breasts when no one else was around. She once aimed her old guns at me and began to lift her blouse. Thankfully, my mom entered the room and Milly quickly pulled down her chemise all the while staring me down with a threatening look that said: "Next time you won't be so lucky." She usually spent time with us around the holidays, and to this day I associate both Christmas and Easter with her enormous, sagging, naked breasts. No wonder I'm not a fan of organized religion.

Chapter 7

Celebrities and
Other Addictions

*"Just because you got the monkey off your back
doesn't mean the circus has left town."*
—GEORGE CARLIN

Celebrity is a most seductive vampire. He is often wealthy, glamorous and devastatingly beautiful. It's a shame that he doesn't show up on film.

There's no denying that we live in a celebrity-obsessed society. The media is on the rich, the famous and the infamous like a mustache on a porn star. As a former entertainment show host who is now a resident of Malibu, California, I have no shortage of celebrity encounters. In Malibu, Tony Danza is more likely to fall from the sky than raindrops (sweetheart of a guy, by the way). Hell, *I'm* also trying to become a celebrity. I already have several agents, a publicist, a personal trainer, a Kabbalah string, an entourage, and a place by the beach. I figure an actual career can't be too far off.

You can see why celebrity is such a beguiling vampire. There are many fabulous perks to being famous. When Britney Spears was asked about the benefits of hitting the big time, she answered: "I get to go to overseas places, like Canada."

Once again, I must repeat that celebrities are for entertainment purposes only and should never eclipse our own real lives. Only you can be the star of your own movie. No one should lose themselves entirely by living vicariously through the rich and famous. If left unchecked, celebrity and its trappings can also blindfold, bind and imprison you. Although this sounds like good kinky fun, you don't want to become a slave to the notorious VIP master.

It's also evident that tabloid culture is out of control with voyeurism reaching creepy proportions. Fame is a drug whether you're obsessed with the famous or seeking your own fifteen minutes, and it should be absorbed in moderation.

This brings us to the most dangerous and cruelest of all vampires: addictions, in all their various shape-shifting forms. There are the obvious addictions like drugs, alcohol, gambling, etc., and the less obvious ones like craving praise and the approval of others, overspending, and never being able to sign off Facebook. There are also the addictions I don't quite understand, like sex addicts. Isn't that every guy? Is it like being addicted to cigarettes? Do sex addicts have sex after they have sex? Are they "jonesing" so badly after a long flight that the moment they land they just grab a baggage handler whom they ravage in customs? I just don't want to know what the sex addict patch looks like.

Personally, in the past my addictions have included diet Red Bull, rage, and nicotine. Ah yes, Nico, as I call him, my smoldering on-and-off-again Latin lover. He was a very demanding and abusive boyfriend.

Here's the deal. I'm not a doctor and I don't think I've ever played one on TV. All I know for sure is that addiction is a killer vampire that devastates and obliterates lives. She is the most powerful and deadly succubus. Don't invite her in. If her evil is already darkening your life, do not attempt to defeat her by yourself. You'll need help stabbing this demon in the heart with a wooden stake.

Star war stories

"A celebrity is a person who works hard all his life to become well-known, then wears dark sunglasses to avoid being recognized."
—FRED ALLEN

Throughout the years, I have brushed tanned, toned shoulders with various celebrities. I have had the privilege of interviewing everyone from Sir Paul McCartney to Dame Edna. I've worked with Samuel L. Jackson and Joan Rivers, made the funny with Jon Stewart and Ray Romano, and I've seen more red carpets than Lindsay Lohan's girlfriend.

A few years back I interviewed Aerosmith, and Steven Tyler hit on me. Now, I realize that this puts me in a club that's about as exclusive as a Costco membership, but it's true nonetheless. I think we formed a bond while arguing over who was the superior Stooge: Curly or Shemp. Steven was bestowing Curly's virtues while I argued that Shemp was the seldom-heralded thinking woman's Stooge. When the interview wrapped, he screamed, "Wait up Miss Canada!" and followed me to craft services. I think he asked for my phone number but I remember little else about the conversation. I just know that he had a boatload of charisma, and that the entire time he was chatting me up I was examining his long, thick wavy hair, his full pouty lips, and his skinny little ass. I wasn't sure if I wanted to do him or be him.

When I was an entertainment anchor for the evening news

in Toronto, we would sometimes report live from various locations in the city. One night the main anchors were going to check in with me on remote at a Planet Hollywood opening. I was standing next to Steven Seagal on a small five-foot stage in the middle of the restaurant. Naturally, I was wearing a pair of my five-inch-high hooker heels. I am always in high heels. In fact, I wear heels so often that my feet have now become permanently arched like Barbie's. Just as the camera's red light came on indicating that we were live to air, one of my heels got caught and I began to fall backwards off the stage. Fortunately, Mr. Seagal caught me in his arms and gingerly placed me back on my feet next to him.

Finally last year, I went to the Malibu Cinemas with my brother Rick and writing partner Paul to see a movie over the Christmas holidays. After the flick finished, I retired to the ladies' room after polishing off a large Diet Coke that was roughly the size of a toddler. Adam Sandler had also decided to spend the night at the movies, and he apparently grew impatient waiting for his wife. While I was in a stall, Adam kicked open the main door to the bathroom and screamed his wife's name at the top of his lungs. This must have startled me because I nervously let out a little toot. Well, I was in the *loo* after all. Besides, I believe Adam is a fan of scatological humor.

In summary, I've flirted with a rock star, was saved by an action hero, and farted in front of a comedian. That's the thing about celebrities; you just have to know how to behave appropriately around each one of them.

Up in smoke and mirrors

"Every form of addiction is bad, no matter whether the narcotic be alcohol or morphine or idealism."

—CARL GUSTAV JUNG

Ty and I used to live next door to a retired firefighter named Don, which made us feel safe during L.A.'s dreaded fire season. After graduating from a hypnotherapy course, Don needed practicum hours and offered to help me quit smoking once and for all by using hypnotherapy. When we met, Don was in his mid-sixties and seemed a wicked combination of manly man and spiritual advisor.

Don and I became fast friends, and he also nicely fulfilled a desperately needed father role in my life. Not only did we see each other for weekly hypnotherapy sessions, we also began a ritual of meditating together every morning. Sometimes I would pop next door and sometimes he would join Ty and me at our place.

I adored Don and looked forward to our time together. I saw him as a bright light and my personal protector. Don taught me about how powerful our subconscious is, and how it's responsible for 88 percent of our decisions. He recommended that I write out all my affirmations and desires by hand every morning and every night to help manifest my dreams more quickly. I had also drastically cut back on the butts.

Don expressed that he would love to join Ty and me some mornings for coffee. A thrice married but now single man, he explained that he missed the company in the early a.m. hours. We happily obliged, and he joined us the next day.

When we all had coffees in hand, Don said that he was anxious to talk to us about something. He wanted to put shock collars on our dogs. I started to laugh because I assumed he was joking. Trust me, our dogs are pretty damn quiet. Besides, Don had a parrot that was louder than both of our dogs combined, and often emitted horrid squeals that sounded like a three-year-old being strangled. Sadly, Don was serious and explained that he didn't like the dogs barking whenever he was at our door. I explained to Don that the dogs were doing their jobs by protecting us. I also told Don that shock collars were completely out of the question. I remember going upstairs after he left and bursting into tears over his inappropriate suggestion. I even decided to be open and talk to Don about how upset his proposal had made me. He assured me that he had been a dog owner all his life, and that he was sorry he had mentioned it.

Months passed and all was well in the neighborhood until one Friday evening when the dogs and I had returned from our beach walk and were greeted by a hideous smell the moment we stepped in the door. I surmised that the foul odor was coming from Don's house. When the stink had persisted for a few hours, I decided to leave Don a phone message alerting him that something might be wrong at his place. A gas leak? An ammonia spill? I wasn't sure, but I told him in the message that I was getting worried about him, and that my eyes were burning and I was feeling nauseous. Even though I closed all the windows, I became quite ill.

I was still sleeping when Don called inquiring as to whether or not we would be meditating together. I bowed out explaining that I had been sick all night, and later that day Don came over saying he owed me an apology and an explanation. He then proceeded to show me his front lawn, which now displayed what appeared to be hundreds of mothballs. Our lawns were tiny, maybe four by six feet, and I was still perplexed. Don said the smell was from the mothballs, and that he had probably overdone it. He went on to point out that mothballs were not only a deterrent to moths, but they were also effective at keeping dogs at bay. Apparently, Don wasn't crazy about Buster's occasional whiz on his prized lawn. He had never mentioned anything to us prior to this, so I found the entire mothball napalming to be a bit extreme. I was also confused as to why he hadn't returned my call the night before when I was concerned about him and suffering through the wretched smell.

Armed with several Internet printouts warning of the severe toxicity of mothballs (ingested or inhaled) Ty and I kindly asked Don to remove all of the retro pesticide from his lawn. I was also terrified that one of the dogs or a neighborhood child had taken a fancy to one of the bright, shiny white balls. Don seemed to have a bit of a cowboy attitude while talking to me, and the smirk on his face combined with my over-protective nature where my dogs are concerned caused me to lose my proverbial shit. I told him, in no uncertain terms, that he had endangered both us and our dogs, and that neutered pets weren't responsible for yellow spots on a lawn; droughts were. Through teary eyes, I kept repeating how I thought we were friends and still couldn't grasp why he didn't just talk to us if he was bothered by our dogs. He returned that I had dismissed the shock collar idea so he had stepped up his game.

It's not that I don't respect someone else's property, but I will never understand how someone could value a tiny lawn over a cherished friendship. Even though he apologized and we let the incident go, things were never the same between Don and me, and I stopped the hypnotherapy sessions. Maybe it's just me, but I'm not comfortable being put under by anyone who may secretly want to kill my dogs.

Don is not really at fault here. He is a kind man who taught me a great deal. The biggest lesson I learned from Don was that smoking wasn't my only addiction. I had to face the fact that for years I had been desperately searching for someone who wouldn't let me down, someone who would watch over me, someone I could feel safe with... In essence, a protective male role model. So desperate was I to find this that whenever George Michael sang Father Figure, I would call him Daddy! The hard truth is that we have to be our own saviors. We also have to make our own peace with our fathers or anyone else who is troubling us. Most of all, we have to let it go.

This incident was another reminder that I tend to get close to people and bring them fully into my life at breakneck speed. I could use a boundary or two.

I'm happy to report that I am no longer on a quest for a father figure, and that I no longer smoke. Now if I could just stop mainlining Vicodin in the bathroom, I'd be all set.

Chapter 8

Sycophants, Svengalis &
Obsessive Repulsives

"Passion is a positive obsession. Obsession is a negative passion."
—PAUL CARVEL

This final and seemingly random grouping of vampires all share one common goal: To keep your ego front and center and to block you from any type of responsibility or humiliation. The ass-kissers are obvious yes-men vampires who only whisper into your ear what you want to hear and continue to feed your ego until it gets so fat they can feast on it for eternity. Remember, these hypocrites always follow their own agenda and never have your best interests at heart. It's much better to surround yourself with honest, non-sycophantic friends who push you to become your most authentic self. Nothing good ever comes from anyone blowing smoke up your ass. All this does is make your sphincter cough. Ass-kissers are weak little weasels. End of story.

Svengalis are only interested in transforming you into their own image. They want to create a clone of their own ego. Svengali vampires are generally successful and charismatic; they are often older and commanding. But come on, anyone who uses *The Art of War* to get into your pants should not be trusted.

Svengalis take away your ability to be unique because they mold you into miniature versions of themselves or make you into an appendage. It's ironic that this type of vampire wants a reflection of himself when vampires can't see their own reflection.

Also, Svengalis are always supremely controlling and often abusive. I have been engaged six or seventeen times, and I can tell you with absolute certainty that fiancé number three was the Svengali poster child.

Sheldon rocked my romantic world and dazzled me with his savvy and intellect. A suave and accomplished older man, he put me so high up on a pedestal that I needed an oxygen mask. He slapped an engagement ring on my finger that was worth more than the GNP of Lichtenstein, vowed to make me happy for the rest of my life, and completely swept me off my feet. The problem with being swept off your feet is that you no longer have your own two legs to stand on. Once he had claimed me as his soon-to-be wife, Sheldon proceeded to isolate me from family and friends, demanded that I change my personality, and verbally abused me so severely that I stopped eating for weeks. When my self-esteem dropped lower than my weight and everyone dear to me staged an intervention, I finally left him. I never danced with a Svengali again because I still have the faint scars from where he bit into my neck and I lost a lot of blood. (*Note:* I changed his name because he is a lawyer!)

Never confuse obsession with love. If someone is obsessed with you, it's not romantic—it's a disorder. For a long time I mistook obsession for love. I thought that if a guy wasn't completely obsessed with me, he didn't care for me. But after discovering someone has been hired to follow you; walking in on someone sniffing your fishnets; catching someone standing over your bed watching you sleep; it all begins to get old and deeply disturbing. Obsessive-repulsives are vampires fixated on you. Even Wikipedia defines obsession as an unhealthy fixation. Destruction follows obsession, and that's not the next level on the food chain anyone should aspire to. No one should dominate your thoughts, nor should you constantly occupy another's. This is yet another form of addiction. Don't get hooked.

All of the vampires in this sub-section circle you and keep you in what I have coined "The Comfort Twilight Zone," a horrible safe-house where your ego will never let you risk humiliation. Here's one of the secrets of the Universe: humiliation is your friend and your liberator. Once you've suffered through a little and survived it intact, you realize that it's no big deal. Ridicule leaves you with nothing to lose and frees you from the opinions of others. Kabbalists believe that one solid humiliation is equal to a year of fasting. They believe that it lifts your soul higher. After the countless humiliations I have endured in my life, I should be able to fly. In fact, I should actually be orbiting the earth.

The naked truth

"Why don't I come up and see you sometime when you're in the nude...
I mean mood."

—SHEMP HOWARD

Throughout high school I worked at a women's clothing store in Guelph, Ontario called Flair. It was owned by a wonderful couple, Madeleine and Karl. They were my first bosses and I was lucky enough to be under the tutelage of two exceptional, beautiful and warm people.

Mad and Karl took the time and patience to teach me about the clothing industry, and they instilled in me a phenomenal work ethic that I believe I carry to this day. Working for this couple also ignited my passion for fashion, and although it was just a part-time gig, they treated me like family. They put up with all my adolescent shenanigans, including the time I rallied the other part-time high school student (a quiet, blonde, timid lass) and convinced her to march with me into Karl's office and demand what I felt was a long overdue raise. Fortunately, Karl interpreted my rudeness and insolence as drive, and, to fuel my ambition, eventually made me night manager of the store.

Karl is originally from Germany and speaks with an accent. Madeleine is from Newfoundland, Canada and also speaks with an accent... just kidding! They are madly in love and have been together forever.

Throughout the years I worked in their store they often spoke of their "cottage." Apparently, it cost money to even visit their campsite, and until I was nineteen-years-old, where they resided remained a bit of a mystery to me. Finally, they divulged that they lived in a nudist colony just outside town. The irony was not lost on me—the two owners of a clothing store were nudists! I was intrigued, and they let me know that I was always welcome.

Cut to: I loved spending time in the nudist colony. From my first visit, I found it to be a fabulous atmosphere where I felt completely safe and uninhibited. In fact, I brought several of my friends to the "nature" resort. My best buddy from high school, Stephanie, came with me to a baby shower there where more than one naked woman was pregnant: very Demi Moore circa 1991. I brought my university roommate to the resort where we played volleyball in the pool against a group of naked cherubs. I also paraded a couple of boyfriends through the resort, and played nude ping pong with my then-boyfriend John. Of course, he won— he had the advantage. I even celebrated my twenty-first birthday chez Mad and Karl's—fully clothed of course. (If you're keeping track, all this happened while I was still a virgin!)

The nudist colony regulars were European and much older than me, so I never felt ill at ease. Besides, the residents (and guests) were only naked in the pool area or while sunbathing, etc. I still cherish hilarious images of a man called Hans getting off his motorcycle in the parking lot completely naked except for his leather boots. I also giggled when I witnessed the all-nude (except for white tennis shoes) doubles match—very difficult to keep your eye on the ball. But my favorite memory was watching Karl's son Henry fixing the roof wearing nothing but a tan, a smile, and a tool belt.

Although I haven't seen Mad and Karl for awhile, they attended my thirtieth birthday party and my first wedding. I haven't been back to the club *au naturel* since I was twenty-one.

I know some people get uptight about this sort of thing, but it sure seemed a hell of a lot more civilized than all the violence our culture is so enamored with. I still fail to understand why Americans have absolutely no problem with seventy-eight people meeting heinous, graphic deaths during the opening credits of a movie, but yet freak out at the site of a nipple. The nudist colony in Southern Ontario is just a European-style resort where sun worshippers and their families share a community. I remember everyone I met there very fondly, and am very grateful to Mad and Karl for bringing me into their world.

I am sharing this story to stress the importance of opening one's mind to new adventures, and pushing beyond one's comfort zone. The thing is, I'm comfortable being naked. I love it. I'm naked right now as I write this.

Stage fright

"If life is just a stage, then we are all running around ad-libbing with absolutely no clue what the plot is. Maybe that's why we don't know whether it's a comedy or tragedy."
—BILL WATTERSON

At the age of three, I performed in my first tap dance recital in Sault Ste. Marie. I was taking lessons from an accomplished dancer by the name of Helen Syjut. I believe, at that time I was her youngest student. In my debut number, I played the caboose of a train in an ensemble piece. As the legend goes, upon completion of the dance routine the crowd erupted into generous and supportive applause. Apparently, I found this quite delicious and refused to exit offstage with the other dancers. Drunk with power and delight, I remained onstage and continued to wave to the crowd, pose for pictures and curtsy until Mrs. Syjut came onstage and carried me away. So my first performance was as a delusional caboose; and you could argue that I have continued to make an ass of myself onstage ever since.

At times, I wish I had remained a dancer instead of attempting comedy. I have done stand-up at some rather unusual venues. I've performed comedy at two wakes and a funeral. I've done a solid twenty minutes at a sex-toy party. And I was the feature act at a retirement home. I killed. Literally.

The fundraisers seem to produce the most bizarre shows. I emceed a night in Toronto to raise awareness for the exotic dancers' union, and to raise money for an animal shelter. I co-hosted a bingo night at a bar in West Hollywood with a drag queen called Brigitte of Madison County. I also flew to Edmonton, Alberta to perform comedy to a room of two hundred men in order to raise money for prostate cancer. Admittedly, I know very little about this type of cancer, and when I asked my husband about it on the way to the airport, he informed me that if the prostate is stimulated, men orgasm. My first question to the all-male crowd was, "Why the hell aren't you having your prostates checked on a weekly basis?" They should be going for second and third opinions. Early detection is the key.

Recently, I got booked to do a fundraiser for Alcoholics Anonymous. I guess I didn't get as many details as I should have because I ended up putting on a fancy dress and asking my gay best friend Kevin if he would throw on a suit and be my escort for the evening.

We drove from L.A. to San Pedro, and discovered that the show was taking place in a very rough part of town, in what looked to be an abandoned Legion hall. Since we arrived way ahead of time, Kevin and I decided to go for a drink before the show. We pulled into the parking lot of what looked to be a fine establishment, but quickly turned around and exited when we spotted a large, unruly man spread-eagled and handcuffed across the hood of a cop car.

We found a nearby Mexican restaurant and both proceeded to knock back Margaritas the size of Smart Cars. We then began the slow march toward the shanty Legion hall. The place looked pretty sketchy, and everyone was scattered outside drinking coffee and smoking. I had just quit and needed to get away from the temptation, so Kevin and I just stood frozen in the far corner of the lot wearing our Sunday best and feeling like idiots. I had even donned a whimsical hat for the evening's festivities.

I won't lie to you, most of the crowd looked like they had just been released from prison. Piercings were abundant and teeth were scarce. It was basically a halfway house, and the attendees were very excited that a comedy night had been organized for their entertainment. Everyone stared at me like I was some exotic animal who had just escaped from the zoo. I was also aware that I was now present at an AA function and most likely reeked of tequila.

The first two comics went to the front of the room and did their acts without any hitches. The emcee announced my name and I began playing with the audience and doing my act. All was going surprisingly well until a somewhat zaftig and disheveled woman came through the door and grabbed a seat next to Kevin. Suddenly, I became aware that this woman was talking rather loudly during my routine. I couldn't quite make out what she was saying because she appeared to have the rational clarity of a drunken Gary Busey. She was slurring, barking out random commands at me, and flirting aggressively with Kevin.

Usually I can handle a heckler—no problem. But I wasn't about to attack this poor woman at an AA event. I didn't know if this was part of the drying out process or one of her steps, so I let it go. Then I went right into a gay joke and basically outed Kevin to everyone there. Upon hearing this information, the Rubenesque woman jumped out of her seat, hit my friend in the arm and yelled, "YOU'RE GAY?" When she sat back down on her seat, a giant zip lock bag full of vodka fell out of her dress and splashed all over the floor. She was immediately removed and I was able to finish the funny without any further interruptions.

All in all, the evening was a success. The audience was lovely and very appreciative. When we returned to the Mexican restaurant our car still had its tires, and a man wearing a jaunty pork pie hat and sporting a tattoo of an eagle across his chest asked both Kevin and me out.

CARE AND TREATMENT OF YOUR

Vampires

❱ Do not feed your vampires.

❱ Do not let a vampire overstay his welcome. If he makes a mess of your life or your place, remember that cold water, Febreze and lemon juice will get rid of most blood stains and that nasty rotting vampire smell.

❱ If you feel your vampire is getting too strong, do not worry. He is easily defeated. When you think about it, an Amish dude has the necessary tools to kick a vampire's ass. Just locate a wooden stake, a crucifix or some garlic. Hell, an out-of-control vampire can be finished off with one good Caesar salad.

❱ Don't be fooled by vampire trickery. This is not your ultimate mate. The vampire doesn't even have a cool superpower; all he can do is turn into a bat. Think about it—what sane woman actually wants a boyfriend who morphs into something that fucks up her hair?

❱ A good doorman can effectively cock block your average vampire.

❱ Don't spend too much time in the dark with your vampire; he will have the advantage. Try to schedule time with your vampire while the sun is still up. Most vampires lose their allure in the light of day.

❱ If bitten, fight the urge to turn into a vampire yourself.

❱ Do not let a vampire sweep you off your feet. It's impossible to turn yourself around once you're in the fireman's carry no matter how hard you try. Sure, being in a vampire's arms will spare your stilettos, but instead of saving the soles of your shoes, save your actual soul.

> ❭ Don't allow yourself to become jaded after a few
> experiences with vampires. See them for what they
> are and try to learn the lesson. Just because you've
> had brushes with the undead doesn't mean you have
> to become dead inside.

> ❭ Don't let your vampire lull you into a false sense of
> security with his sweet talk and promises of eternal
> life. Just keep in mind that vampires are nothing more
> than sponges with better PR.

> ❭ If you want to ward off a vampire, prayer never hurts. You
> could even play Duran Duran's Save a Prayer for Me Now, as
> Duran Duran will ward off pretty much everyone.

> ❭ Anger is also a very destructive vampire. Although this
> may sound trite, "anger" is just one consonant away
> from "danger". Keep that in mind.

> ❭ If you feel you are in the presence of a vampire who
> is draining your energy, surround yourself with white
> light. You could even surround yourself with white
> trash... Whatever works for you.

PART III

Douche Bags

douche bag [**d**oo**sh** b**a**igh]
—*noun*

1. *a small syringe having detachable nozzles for fluid injections, used chiefly for vaginal lavage and for enemas.*

2. *slang: an unattractive or offensive person.*

"You can't change someone's mind if they don't have one."
—BILL MAHER

My own definition tends to lean towards the second dictionary explanation, and expands on it. Douche bags are the people and things in our world that may not necessarily be life-threatening or altering, but which can sabotage our progress and make our day-to-day lives more negative, painful, and definitely less fulfilling. Notice that I also include *things* in this category because places, events and circumstances can be douchy too.

Douche bag is a term that applies to both men and women. However, female douche bags are also commonly referred to as "douche hags" or "douche baguettes." Furthermore, douchism does not have an age limit. Kids can act like douche bags (these are known as "douche nuggets"), and the elderly are not exempt when it comes to displaying douche tendencies either. There are particularly grumpy old dudes (douche fossils) who are clearly suffering through *man*opause. They are constantly subjecting us to their hateful, intolerant and narrow-minded views by being impatient and complaining about everything.

Although the expression "douche bag" appears to be an integral part of the modern vernacular, the slang usage of this derogatory term dates back to the 1960s. Who could forget the classic 1980 *Saturday Night Live* skit featuring Buck Henry and Gilda Radner as Lord and Lady Douchebag?

The word "douche" has its roots in the French language and means "shower." This is appropriate because once you've spent some time in the company of a douche bag, that's exactly what you want to go home and do. Personally, I adore the expression "douche bag" because whenever I hear it, it never fails to make me giggle, which immediately takes the sting out of anyone acting like a douche.

Douche bags are often more transparent and easier to spot than your average angel or vampire, but behaving like a douche has become the norm for too many people. In fact, being reactive, thoughtless, arrogant and petty is classic douche bag behavior that has become far too acceptable these days.

If you are having difficulty distinguishing between a vampire and a douche bag, I believe my husband put it best when he said, "George Bush is douche bag, and Dick Cheney is a vampire." Sure, Dick may seem to have more power and be more dangerous and threatening, but douchebaggery left unchecked and unchallenged can have its own disastrous repercussions. Plus, douches are freakin' annoying!

It's obvious that we are currently living in a douche bag culture if the dozens of Internet sites dedicated to this phenomenon are any indication. Douchebagitis is reaching epic proportions, with celebrity douche bags like Jon Gosselin, Kevin Federline, Michael Lohan, and the douchecasters at Fox News being constantly glorified in all the tabloids and entertainment shows. Douche bags can be found in every arena: sports, music, politics, law, etc., and they seem to be thriving in an ideal breeding ground.

Here are some physical attributes that will help you identify a douche bag. Any one of these traits does not necessarily a douche bag make; but if someone you know exhibits a handful or more, then to paraphrase an idiom from Blue Collar uber-comedian Jeff Foxworthy—you might know (or be) a douche bag.

The male douche bag's uniform consists of the mandatory wife-beater undershirt, or a shirt so tight that one suspects it was ripped off the back of a stolen G.I. Joe doll. These douches are also fond of wearing pastel Izod shirts featuring starched collars in the upright position. (*Note:* These should never be worn unless the person in question owns a time machine and makes frequent visits back to 1983.)

Douche burgers are prone to over-accessorizing with gold statement-pendants engraved with words like "Baddass" or "Daddy," bracelets that ponder, "Who Would Jesus Do?" and gaudy pinky rings the size of a baby's head. Male douches also fancy fur coats. It must be made clear that unless your name is Huggy Bear or you are a Russian explorer, you should never don a fur coat. The Douchley-do-Right also sports a spray-on tan in such a hideous shade of orange not found in nature, that it looks as though a spilled bag of renegade Cheetos had on orgy on his chest. The male douche bag puts so much gel and product in his hair that he could easily take a sniper's bullet or power a diesel engine car. He can also frequently be seen driving a Hummer with vanity plates that declare: "IM469".

The typical douche hag has a signature look that marries douchy and hoochie like no other. The female douche is fond of ill-fitting clothing that exposes almost every erogenous zone on her body and displays her plethora of tattoos. These tattoos are often written in Asian characters, Aramaic or Sanskrit; and although the douche baguette thinks they mean "peace" or "namaste," I suspect many a tattoo artist has messed with these poor douchettes. What is actually stamped on their skin for eternity is "whore" or "anal sex forever." The douche hag also has a penchant for wearing feather earrings and poorly-constructed kaleidoscopic hair extensions; and she doesn't shy away from wearing six-inch stiletto heels with cut-off jean shorts or bikinis. She favors Bedazzled tube tops or statement t-shirts that ask: "Got MILF?" across her breasts. Or one which broadcasts her life credo: "I don't come from money, I come because of it!" La femme douche generally couples these t-shirts with hostile tight white pants that often result in a prominent camel toe. She is also prone to wearing several layers of foundation and mascara en route to the gym. The *pièce de résistance* is dark brown lip-liner so generously applied it's as if her mouth was dead and she was providing a chalk outline to announce this fact.

Both male and female douche bags are also prone to wearing sunglasses 24/7. They don their sunglasses indoors, at night, in the shower, and while they have sex. Sorry, but only Bono is allowed to wear sunglasses all the time.

Certain personality traits are inherent in many garden-variety douche bags. For instance, they are typically quite narcissistic. Douche bags will speak incessantly about themselves even though the topic at hand may be the stockpiling of Iran's nuclear weapons or global warming. They have a special gift of somehow making everything relate to their own lives.

As human beings, it is only natural that at some point we will all disagree, argue and battle over certain issues. What distinguishes douche bags is that they will fight outside their own weight division. By this I mean a CEO who berates an intern, a group of snooty "ladies who lunch" treating a waiter like dirt, or a Little League soccer coach who screams at one of his players. Stick to your own weight class.

There are also varying degrees of douchedom, so I have created a douche Richter Scale for identification purposes:

Minor Offense Douche Violators: The people who send out those threatening chain e-mails, don't pick up after their dogs, or pee on toilet seats.

Misdemeanor Douches: The ones who let the air out of your tires, hit on your girlfriend, or cut you off on a busy highway.

Felony Douche Perpetrators: Douches who sleep with your wife, embezzle money from charities, or kick puppies.

Douche bags come in all types and sizes, and they are everywhere. If we don't take immediate action, they will take over completely. Douche bags need to be called out, avoided at all cost; and when warranted—bitch-slapped out of their Ed Hardy hoodies.

Chapter 9

Mean and Lean

*(Bully douche bags, and extreme diet and
exercise douche rats)*

"Nothing is more despicable than respect based on fear."
—ALBERT CAMUS

Usually the most hurtful and harmful douche bags (to others, and ultimately to themselves) are the cruel bully douche bags. These douches often act in a violent, mean or offensive manner as a result of a horrible childhood. Ironically, they make many of our childhoods horrible in the process. Bullying is a learned behavior that often stems from profound insecurity and/or the continued ugly cycle of having been bullied by parents or others themselves. As Tyra Banks once said, "Hurt people hurt." I can't believe I'm quoting Tyra Banks either, consequently outing myself as a fan of *America's Next Top Model*. What can I say? It's one of my guilty pleasures, and I'm not hurting anyone.

Bullying is undoubtedly a base and animalistic form of communication and intimidation. Haven't we evolved beyond this Cro-Magnon behavior? Whenever you beat the crap out of someone with your fists, words or actions, don't you just end up feeling like a steaming pile of Serbian manure later on? Making fun of people and deliberately trying to hurt them or coerce them through violent threats never elevates bullies. After a while, it just makes them feel pathetic. Perhaps this childish and antediluvian conduct is forgivable when the bully's age is in the single digits, but adult bullies are loitering on the lowest rung of Dante's Hell. People who rely on bullying in order to instill fear, seek revenge or obtain what they want, typically tend to have an IQ lower than room temperature.

There are several ways to manage a bully. First of all, you can stand up to said bullies and confront them. For those of us who avoid confrontation like we avoid colonoscopies, this often doesn't seem like a viable option. However, if the whole law of attraction theory is to be believed, we brought these bullies into our lives, so maybe it's time for us to cowboy-up and tell them that their uncivilized, menacing conduct won't be tolerated. Secondly, never ever live in fear. It signals the death of your freedom. Once you find the proverbial balls to stand up to a heinous bully, this pattern of bullies appearing in your life will soon dissipate. Next, you can also dismiss the bullies and not give them any attention or energy, thus causing them to eventually dry up like the slugs that they are. And finally, you can sweet talk the bullies into submission. Many just need some love... or a good lay.

Bullies are to be pitied, but they cannot be completely ignored. Bullying has become a very serious problem in schools today and has led to tragic consequences. If you suspect your child or friend is being bullied, get involved. If you are suffering at the hands of a bully douche bag, seek help. There should be a bully support group in every community, or at the very least, a giant anti-bully super robot who is programmed to take care of these bastards in an efficient high tech manner so that we don't have to deal with them at all. I have a rich and ambitious fantasy of what the future holds. I just hope that hover boots will be available with high heels.

"I never worry about diets. The only carrots that interest me are the number you put on a diamond."
—MAE WEST

It goes without saying that proper nutrition and exercise are vital to a healthy and happy life. In fact, bullies would do well to cut back on sugar and spend more time doing extracurricular sports. However, if you take dieting and exercising to the extreme, you may find yourself acting like a Douchy McGee. The two biggest culprits in this douche category are men who abuse steroids and white women who refuse to celebrate their bodies. It's true, when was the last time you heard a white woman say, "I'm juicy!"?

Face it dudes—demon 'roids are illegal. They turn you into a freak and shrink your nads! Is it really worth looking like Carrot Top just so that you can enter competitions and dead lift 3,000 pounds with what looks to be popcorn topping slathered all over your body? Ladies, stop following every trendy bullshit diet that hits the market. I'm on the Authentic South Beach Diet—nothing but cocaine and bronzer! Let's try to accept and embrace our bodies as opposed to punishing ourselves when we miss one of our five daily extreme Pilates classes. There is no need for a beautiful grown woman to lose so much weight that she ends up with the body of a twelve-year-old boy with polio.

Be reasonable. Eat real food that isn't made out of ingredients Mensa members can't pronounce. Avoid killer sugars and starches, and load up on fruits and vegetables. Also, suck back a few waters everyday—minus the scotch, of course.

Make every attempt to avoid turning into a douche queen when ordering in a restaurant. It is cringeworthy to witness tiny, pretentious actresses ask a poor waiter if the organic salad dressing they ordered is made with virgin's tears, unicorn milk, and the musk of a Minotaur.

Finally, get up off your ass and squeeze some form of exercise in every day. It doesn't have to be some horrible kick box fusion cardio funk-abs-buster disco-spin class, where a perky instructor the size of Hangman on speed wearing a fuchsia spandex onesy barks out commands. Find something you like to do, and do it more often. Dance, walk on the beach; make whoopie on the dryer. Straight up, you have to do some type of physical activity if you want to keep your heart beating and live long enough to see Chicago host the Olympics or a professional Toronto sports team make it into the playoffs. Besides, you need to stay in shape to stand up to, or outrun bullies.

The loser, by a nose

"If you aren't in over your head, how do you know how tall you are?"

—T.S. ELLIOT

I'm pretty sure that I was an average-to-cute kid; but let me tell you that as an adolescent, I was aggressively ugly. Honestly, there were a few rough years when I looked like the result of a three-way involving Geddy Lee, Howard Stern and Big Bird. I had long, dark curly hair so big and wide I could have deducted it as a dependent on my income tax form.

During the summer between Grades 6 and 7, I shot up to 5' 9" and weighed in at roughly ninety pounds. Whenever I went out in public, I looked like a newborn giraffe stepping into the wild for the first time. I was more awkward than small talk the morning after a one-night stand.

I remember the first Junior High dance I attended after my unwelcome growth spurt. I spent most of the evening sitting alone or with a handful of other misfits until one brave soul approached me from the distance. His name was Shaun Flynn. He was blond and smelled like sunshine, and came up to me and asked me to dance. I remember that moment as being an intoxicating mixture of excitement, fear and elation; until I stood up. I slowly rose above Shaun Flynn like a giant mushroom cloud. I'm sure his body temperature dropped a few degrees in my shadow. Shaun looked up at me and quietly proclaimed, "I'm sorry, I can't help you." Then he ran away like a French soldier. "'I'm sorry, I can't help you?'" Did I just walk into Sephora and ask for hemorrhoid cream?

Actually, the worst part of me wasn't my height; it was my ski-slope nose. "Ski slope" is the polite euphemism for what became a more accurate and far crueler nickname: Pig Nose. Kids used to pull down the windows on the bus and scream, "Pig Nose!" at me as I walked home from school. I endured such severe torture during recess and lunch hour that I'm pretty certain these insensitive schoolmates were in violation of the Geneva Convention. If only I had been homeschooled. I lived in a small town, so there was no way to escape this moniker. Even my Uncle Donnie later reminisced about those dark years saying, "Hey Carla, remember when you were just two legs and a nose?" How could I forget? I was scarred for life. However, since I wasn't exactly the popular beauty queen of Junior High, I had ample time to devote to my studies and ended up becoming the nerd who won all of the academic awards (I know; don't act like it's not sexy).

Miraculously, everything changed in Grade 11. I guess I grew into my body and my nose because I can still clearly remember the day when the boys in my Russian history class threw a note onto my desk. Fearing further taunting, I started to shake like Rush Limbaugh at a gay pride parade while I gingerly opened the folded piece of paper. To my surprise, the note read: "Dear Bambi, we love you." It was signed, "The Young Bucks." I have never known the exact reason why my nickname went from Pig Nose to a stripper's handle, but I distinctly remember feeling a great sense of relief and somehow knowing that my awkward phase was likely a thing of the past.

As crazy as this will sound, I am grateful for that nightmarish period in my life because it made me a much better, more empathetic person. Later that same year, I was sitting with the cool kids in our Grade 11 math class when a new transfer student entered the room. She had a severe underbite and everyone began mocking her. I was horrified and told them to put a stop to it. Trust me, if I hadn't gone through the Pig Nose years, I would never have stepped up.

Soy milking it for all it's worth

"I'd move to Los Angeles if New Zealand and Australia were swallowed by a tidal wave, if there was a bubonic plague in England and if the continent of Africa disappeared from some Martian attack."

—RUSSELL CROWE

People love to take the piss out of L.A. There are thousands of jokes about how Los Angeles is a soulless, plastic and lonely excuse for a city that's as deep as a contact lens. Most women complain that trying to find a decent guy in Hollywood is like trying to find an untouched child in a polygamist colony.

What can I tell you? L.A. is hot, neurotic, a little dirty in parts, and it's constantly rejecting me. So naturally, I'm extremely attracted to it. It's the bad boy of cities.

There are certain truths you glean very quickly after spending a little time in Tinseltown. First, as everyone warns, L.A. is just like high school with money. Second, there are no bad meetings, and the term "good energy" is code for, "I hate your work." Third, the Angelenos have a different sense of fear. None of the usual dangerous suspects seem to disturb them in the least.

Ask anybody in L.A. if they're worried about earthquakes, and you're typically met with this answer: "Oh, I don't even feel them anymore." Apparently, the ever-present threat of shaking earth is remedied by keeping a large supply of bottled water and battery-operated flashlights on hand (which I firmly believe would only save MacGyver's ass!). Bring up the danger of drive-by shootings and you can almost hear the locals' eyes rolling, saying, "Please, that's so ten years ago!"

Even wildfires, such as the horrible fires that ravaged Malibu in 2007, are sometimes treated with a certain lackadaisical attitude. When an out-of-control blaze was raging just across the street from us, our surfer-dude neighbors took the opportunity to go surfing. It's true. They rode the waves as heavy dark smoke billowed over the Pacific Ocean. It looked like a scene from *Apocalypse Now: The Next Generation*. However, let it rain and L.A. collapses like a cheap facelift. At the onset of a shower, the residents here scatter from the streets like extras being chased by Godzilla in an old black and white Japanese horror movie. Everyone panics and completely loses any ability to drive. At the first drop of water, meetings, rehearsals, and Brazilian waxing appointments are cancelled. A rainstorm will occupy the first twenty minutes of every local newscast where we are cautioned to stay home and sleep in shifts. Forget a dirty bomb, terrorists need only to set up an intricate, elaborate sprinkler system and a water slide to bring this city to its knees.

L.A. is also a place where you can conceivably wear a bikini twelve months a year. And so the hottest cocktail in Hollywood is not an Apple Martini—it's the Master Cleanse followed by an enema chaser. Here, for the right price, Kim Kardashian's trainer will come to your home and help your Chihuahua lose those unwanted pounds around its midsection. L.A. is the Mecca of health and fitness. Well, more accurately, it's the Mecca of looking good at all cost. Many actresses stay thin by popping bucketfuls of Fen-Phen, jogging twenty-five miles a day, and smoking half a pack of American Spirit cigarettes for dinner. And listen to their rationalization: "They're totally organic and natural. It's like smoking a carrot." You can't entirely blame them. In Hollywood there is constant pressure for everyone to remain eternally youthful and super skinny. Let's face it, a celebrity in California is more likely to be thrown in jail for being overweight than for offing a spouse or making a sex tape with a minor.

Not long ago, I experienced the quintessential L.A. moment. After recording some cartoon voicework in West Hollywood, I decided to reward myself with a tuna melt. I guess I still haven't adjusted to American fast-food serving portions because my tuna melt turned out to be the size of a Toyota Prius. I kindly offered half of my snack to a homeless man who, hand-to-God, replied: "No thank you, I don't eat dairy." Wow! Like I need more rejection in L.A. Then he shook his head, stared at me very disapprovingly and continued, "And neither should you." You haven't lived until you are judged by someone combing his hair with an expired Starbucks card... Only in L.A!

Chapter 10

I Pity the Fool

(Victim douche bags. See also: Drama queen douchie mamas, and excuse douches)

"If you could kick the person in the pants responsible for most of your trouble, you wouldn't sit down for a month."
—THEODORE ROOSEVELT

At one point or another we've all spent too much time getting wasted at a pity party. The key here, like at any party, is not to be the last to leave. After a bad setback, defeat or traumatic incident, who hasn't spent the better part of two weeks sequestered inside their home wearing the same flannel monkey pajamas and watching back-to-back reruns of *Saved by the Bell*—for days on end? During one of these bouts of blue, who hasn't completely shunned the outside world and ignored proper housekeeping and hygiene until they noticed that their own ecosystem was beginning to spring up in the living room? Who hasn't, at some point, felt such a deep, all-encompassing and paralyzing malaise, that, other than setting a couple of hours aside everyday to weep, all they could do was compose sad and painful lyrics in the meager hopes of penning a hit song for Sarah McLachlan? Just me? Well, you know what I'm getting at. We're all allowed one or two of these episodes per life.

Serial victims are definitely douche bags. Perma-victims make a career out of being hard done-by, and never take action or assume responsibility for themselves. They are forever blaming others for their woes. Victim douches never look within for any type of solution, and are constantly looking to the outside for someone to come swashbuckling in and rescue them. Ironically, you can't save anyone who is stuck in the victim mentality. After a while, you just want to smack'em and say, "Hey, Sir FeelSorryforYourselfaLot, the silent movies called and they want their tied-to-the-railroad-tracks scene back. Clara Bow loves your work." Unless you're Joan of Arc, being a martyr is not a badge of honor. It's also so six hundred years ago.

Kissing cousins to victim douche bags are excuse douches. They will invent a bazillion different reasons why they can't be happy or take action. They usually cite a dysfunctional family background as an excuse. Hmm… that's pretty much all of us, non? Other excuses include economics, gender, age, social status, Mercury retrogrades; you name it. Excuse douches will reject any solution offered and summarily dismiss its worthiness and potential effectiveness. An excuse douche holds an honorary doctorate in rationalization.

My dear friend Bernie Safire is yet another angel whom I've met since moving to L.A. He's a shining example of how to be ageless. Bernie is one of the hairdressers in which the movie *Shampoo* was based, and he is a truly remarkable human being. Not only is he just about the sweetest guy I've ever met (and at the age of eighty he still cuts hair in his Malibu salon every day), he can still do a handstand. In 1983, Bernie was the Senior Olympics gymnastic champion. Moreover, he totally out taps me in our tap dance class. He also outclasses the douche bags.

If you truly believe you've been dealt a lousy hand in

the poker game of life, visit the pediatrics ward of any hospital and witness remarkably determined and optimistic children fighting for their lives. Armed with this perspective, trying to find an excuse for not making the most of your life would be like trying to find a nun's G-spot. Make love, not excuses.

Finally, I'll never understand drama queens. Really? Who's got the time? Why create drama? I think organic drama has a way of finding us without much effort on our part. Tell me why it now seems to be trendy or cool to be a drama queen? I blame the douche bags on *The Hills*—of course. I also blame Heidi Montag and Spencer Pratt for the situation in the Middle East and world hunger; and I still don't know who the hell they are! With everything happening in the world today, is it really appropriate to crawl into the fetal position and wail hysterically because the store was out of this season's Prada clutch?

Drama douches blow everything so out of proportion that I'm convinced their minds are made out of fun-house mirrors. They turn minutia into major deals because they absolutely thrive on the theatrical. I know people who claim on a daily basis to be "freaking out," "having a meltdown," or "suffering from a complete nervous breakdown." It's like their mantra. The root causes of these alleged meltdowns usually include anything from receiving the wrong latte at Starbucks to accidentally over conditioning their hair to getting a parking ticket. Get a grip and introduce yourself to reality. The two of you definitely need to spend some quality time together.

Finally, if you're not a celebrated opera star or Beyonce, but label yourself a diva in order to get your own way, belittle others, and act superior to everyone; you're not a diva—you're just a bitch (or a prima doucha).

A front row ticket to the gun show

"There are only two forces in the world, the sword and the spirit.
In the long run the sword will always be conquered by the spirit."
—NAPOLEON BONAPARTE

When I was eleven-years-old, I worked part-time at my father's convenience store. It was located in a VERY small town called Wallaceburg, Ontario. Population: Maybe. Wallaceburg boasted that it was the lacrosse capital of the world. Since I could never fully understand or appreciate the sport of lacrosse, this honor was completely lost on me. It seemed to me like a more violent version of hockey that involved a lot of running with jacked-up butterfly nets.

Early on a Tuesday evening, I was working in my dad's store with a pretty but somewhat sullen sixteen-year-old (ironically named Merilee) when two men wielding guns, their faces covered by nylon stockings, entered the store and screamed, "This is a stick-up!" I have to admit, this nearly made me chuckle. It was so damned cliché. I was in the process of ringing in someone's order and couldn't immediately open my till. The bad guy closest to me, who was conveniently carrying a large sawn-off shotgun, pressed the cold barrel to my forehead and yelled, "Hurry up!" Which I did. I remember thinking that they were going to kill us because on all the prime time television cop shows, the serious criminals wore something to distort their faces only when they planned on offing their victims.

After we handed over the money, the two robbers left

the store and I can remember hearing Merilee sobbing behind me. I was stunned and continued ringing in the customer's order, but stopped when I realized I wouldn't be able to make change for his $20 bill. I told the guy to take the loaf of bread and cigarettes and scram.

Dazed and undoubtedly in shock, I sat back on the tiny stool situated behind the counter. I finally pulled myself together long enough to press a button under the counter that triggered a buzzer in our adjacent home. My father (who had only stepped out of the store long enough to shave) came running in with traces of Gillette foam on his face. When I told him what had happened, he went running after the assailants with a crazed look in his eyes, but the robbers were long gone. When my father returned, I was forced to speak with a series of police officers and fill out a variety of forms. This was a lot to absorb for a Grade 6-er. Later that night, inside the safety of our home, I just kept staring down at my multicolored striped-toe socks, wishing I was somewhere far, far away.

I know it seems like being the victim of an armed robbery would be a life-altering and harrowing experience for a pubescent girl, but in retrospect, I'm grateful I was eleven-years-old when the incident took place. Children are far more resilient. I think if it happened to me now I would have a heart attack; or at the very least drop a deuce in my pants. I would be much more of a victim douche bag now. Fortunately, it barely affected me back then. I didn't even have bad dreams about the robbery. After all, it wasn't so much a near-death experience as a nearby-death experience. No one was hurt, and within a few days a cute boy or a new song on the radio garnered all my attention. That's the wonder of youth and innocence; you just move on and immediately return to your regular scheduled life. If only we could handle situations that arise in our adulthood in the same manner.

The experience definitely imprinted me though. I honestly believe that I became a champ in all future crisis situations in my life as a result of the robbery. We later discovered that the young men who had held us up at gunpoint, did so for drug money. I firmly believe that's the reason why I have never experimented with any type of drug in my life. I've never even smoked a joint. I'm not being judgmental; some of my best friends are lovable potheads. I'm just being factual.

Almost two years later to the day, I was once again working in dad's store when we were robbed at gunpoint a second time. I even had the pleasure of testifying in court about that one. Mercifully, as a result of the second armed robbery, my family moved away from Wallaceburg. Good call. After it had happened twice when I was working, I figured I either had the worst convenience store cashier luck ever, or I was in on the take. If it's the latter, I'm still waiting for my share you drugged out, armed douche bags.

Yes Virginia, there is a superwoman

"A generous heart, kind speech, and a life of service and compassion are things which renew humanity."
—BUDDHA

L ast year, I hosted a fundraiser for a charitable group called Leave Out Violence (LOVE). This organization helps to remove young people from violent situations, and by reaching into schools and communities, teaches teen-agers to make non-violent choices.

The benefit gala was held in Toronto at the beautiful Art Deco Eglinton Theatre on the same night as the Academy Awards. The gist of the evening was to watch the Oscar broadcast as the audience enjoyed live entertainment and delicious nosh. The goal was to raise awareness and funds for LOVE.

My Mom and my friend Bunny came to the event as my dates. It was called "An Evening with Oscar," and I was the emcee. I was asked to do some comedy before the broadcast started as well as introduce some of the people from LOVE who would be speaking about the organization. Remember, this was the first time this particular group had hosted an Oscar evening fundraiser, and I wasn't terribly familiar with LOVE. I noticed that one of the women I was to intro-duce was the founder. She was listed on the program as "Twinkle." Thankfully, I instinctively knew not to make some stupid, cheap joke about her stripper-sounding name. After I introduced Twinkle, and she took the podium, I sat back down at my table in front of the stage between Mom and Bunny.

Twinkle told the story of why she founded LOVE. Back in 1972, Twinkle and Dan, her beloved husband of many years, were driving to dinner with another couple in Mon-treal to celebrate Greek Day. For some reason, they turned down the wrong street. It was on this random street that they witnessed a young boy knock over an elderly lady and steal her purse. Dan chased after the assailant on foot while Twinkle took the wheel and drove the car around the block. By the time Twinkle turned the corner, her husband Dan was already dead. The teenage boy had been carrying a knife and stabbed Dan to death. The police apprehended the attacker who turned out to be a fourteen-year-old boy.

Years after this horrific and senseless act, Twinkle began looking into the boy's background and discovered that he was a runaway from Baltimore who came from a single parent family. His mother worked three jobs and he had been brought up in front of the television. He ran away to Montreal, joined a gang and did a lot of drugs. He had hit the streets that night to steal some money so he could score LSD.

Twinkle said she realized there were two victims on that dark night in Montreal: Her husband, who lost his life attempting to help another, and the young boy who took a precious life as a result of his own depraved and violent upbringing. Twinkle decided that something had to be done to help deeply troubled youth like the lost teenager who killed her husband. So she took action. Twinkle created LOVE to help identify the causes of teen violence and to give young people the courage to change their lives. She wanted to give these kids a voice and an alternative to a life of crime and violence. Twinkle spoke about the importance of saving the lives of these kids who don't have any hope.

I was so blown away by this woman's story, and by the sheer beauty of her heart and spirit, that my jaw dropped and I began to cry. I had to go back on stage and thank her, but I had a very difficult time composing myself. I was so overwhelmed by her unselfishness and her unbelievable capacity for forgiveness, that I just stood there awestruck at the podium. My mom nearly jumped up on stage because she didn't think I could pull myself together. Twinkle could see that I was struggling and suggested that I make a joke. I didn't manage to do that, and I was only able to mumble, "This planet needs more people like you Twinkle."

Months after that evening, I found myself still very deeply affected by this remarkable woman. I had the privilege of speaking to Twinkle not long ago, and she was kind enough to elaborate on her story and share some of her philosophies with me.

Twinkle offered more details about the night her husband was killed, and she explained that it was a magical story in many ways. She told me that her husband had a premonition earlier that day, and that he had wondered aloud, "What would you do without me?" Twinkle had donned a black dress for their Saturday night out on the town (which she added was unusual for her) but her husband had made her take it off, explaining, "I don't want you to look like a widow." She added how she found it interesting that this happened on Greek Day, because it became a Greek tragedy.

Twinkle also divulged that the chief of police, who was a Roman Catholic, took her aside after the horrific incident and told her, "This has nothing to do with our respective religions. It was no accident. This came from a higher place." Twinkle agrees with this, and feels that she is only the vehicle through which the type of work being done by LOVE is possible. She sincerely thinks that she is just a vessel and should not be thanked because her work comes from a higher place. I was overwhelmed by her humility, and decided to ask her exactly how she found the strength and grace to forgive and carry on.

Twinkle acknowledged that it took her some time. Following the heinous incident, she spent many years in total avoidance doing anything that would take her away from it. She said that she had to do a lot of spiritual work on her own life before she could help others, and revealed how she had been living a life that was less than satisfactory before that ill-fated night in Montreal. Twinkle explained that she had been surrounded by bad relationships and was forced to do some housecleaning. The next step, she told me, was recognizing that she had a story to tell.

Twinkle values the art of First Nations storytelling, and how it has been used throughout history to teach lessons. She also admitted that there were times when she wanted to walk away but felt she had a responsibility to inspire others and provide hope to kids who were burdened by violence. Twinkle knew that her personal story could teach young people to forgive and to avoid anger and revenge. She acknowledged that the incident had indeed affected her whole life, but to have remained angry at the boy, she shared, would have ruined her life. Instead, she assured me, he saved her life.

Twinkle advises that when something horrible occurs in our lives, we must look beyond what is happening to us and make sense of it by doing something about it. She claims that if you're a victim, you're not powerful, and therefore empty. Twinkle told me that when we stay in anger or revenge mode we get caught in a web. She feels our job on earth is to get that web to disintegrate.

She considers working with kids to be a blessing and a gift. She thrives on the creativity, the culture, and by watching something grow. Twinkle gushed about the LOVE program's five-day leadership conference that she has been attending for years, and how it has provided her with the best moments of her life. She also graciously offered the following advice: She urges people never to retire, and stresses the importance of remaining engaged in life. Twinkle cautions that if we don't, small details will begin to add up, get us down, and ultimately become painful. She also relies heavily on music and laughter, and I was quite surprised and delighted to discover that this incredible woman has a wicked, dark sense of humor.

After we said our good-byes and made plans to sit together at next year's LOVE fundraiser, I hung up the phone and sat in stillness with a smile on my face for God knows how long. It's odd that I remained so motionless after being so incredibly moved by this woman. I think I was trying to come up with a stronger, more fitting, and more highly evolved title for her than angel. No need. She was already christened Twinkle.

Chapter 11

The C-Word

(Cowardly douches. See also: Judgmental, intolerant, and hater douche bags)

"Hatred is the coward's revenge for being intimidated."
—GEORGE BERNARD SHAW

This particular category will expose the most insidious citizens of Doucheland—the cowardly and hater douche bags.

Cowardly douches often hide behind their prejudices, politics, religion, and the alleged moral majority. They fear intensely anything outside their own comfort zone and philosophies, and are unwilling to accept change or progress because it might affect the douche status quo. They cling desperately to the past where they can safely remain bathing in ignorance. They also appear to pine for the supposed good ol' days, which I'm guessing involves going back to a time when covered wagons were circling, women couldn't vote, and minorities had no rights to speak of, including freedom... No thanks!

Cowardly douches do not subscribe to the unspoken live-and-let-live motto. They immediately reject or denounce any opinion or lifestyle that differs from their own. Seriously, why fear or oppose gay marriage? I am mystified as to why this is even an issue when we live in a society that promises equal rights to all. For the love of Streisand, gay marriage has absolutely no affect on your life or on the sanctity of your heterosexual union. The love between any two people is the same and should offer the same rights and privileges. The only thing that's different is that every gay marriage I have attended has been far superior to any traditional marriage. The music is fantastic, the food outstanding, and the vows original and witty. Just remember to never throw rice at a gay wedding as almost all my gay boyfriends are off carbs. I am a big supporter of gay marriage. I do worry about gay divorce though. Who gets the pug?

The coward douche is often two-faced, acting one way in public then behaving in an entirely different manner when no one is watching. These double-life douches are not to be trusted. Fear and ignorance is a horrible cop buddy movie with little, if any, entertainment value. Aung San Suu Kyi said, "Fear is not the natural state of civilized people." Dorothy Thompson adds that "the most destructive element in the human mind is fear. Fear creates aggressiveness." Fear also creates cowardly douche bags. Just say no to fear.

Unfortunately, we are all familiar with hater douche bags. These people are so negative and critical that they actually may smell of vinegar. Hater douches are terminally negative thinkers and chronic complainers who whine so much you could get drunk just listening to them. By the way, it helps to be drunk while listening to them.

We all know negative douche bags who not only see the glass as half empty, but also bitch about the dishwasher spots on the glass. Overt haters are easy enough to ferret out and avoid, but some douches can be more subtle in their complaints and critiques. If, after spending time with a certain person you feel crappy about yourself and depleted of energy, chances are you've just been in the company of a hater-douche-vampire hybrid. This wicked combo is quite toxic and will not only suck the life out of you, but convince you that life sucks.

Hater douches are disappointed whenever things don't go their way or people refuse to bend to their will. They appear permanently stuck in what Freud called the *id* stage. This behavior is only acceptable when the person in question is two years old. A grumpy adult throwing a tantrum and screaming, "Mine!" is not only a douche, but an effective form of birth control.

If hater douche bags and cowardly douches dropped the fear and swapped complaints for appreciation, not only would they become happier, more connected and evolved human beings, they would get invited to a hell of a lot more parties.

Message bored

"Anyone can negatively criticize—it is the cheapest of all comment because it requires not a modicum of the effort that suggestion requires."
—CHUCK JONES

In recent years, cowardly douches have been armed with a new and powerful weapon they can hide behind which they use for evil instead of good: the Internet. The World Wide Web, YouTube, Facebook, and even e-mail are like heroin for cowardly douches. There is even a cyber term within online communities to describe users who post without a screen name or under a faux name: "Anonymous coward."

Most of us have been cyber-slammed by a known or unknown assailant. One time, a disgruntled ex-wife read a joke on my website and took it upon herself to blast out a warning to everyone in her address book (and many in mine) that I was a porn addict. Admittedly, there are a number of things I can be called out on. But c'mon, if I was a porn addict I'd be on the cover of Time magazine, because I would be the only female porn addict on the planet.

Porn holds no interest for women. First of all, porn flicks use the same horrible fluorescent lighting found in dressing rooms when you're trying on a swimsuit. So out of the gate, it's already traumatizing; plus the hair, wardrobe and makeup are hideous in these films. Guys may be fine with the so-called plots involving slutty nurses and horny pizza delivery boys, but women just can't suspend belief in that way. We're realists. Nurses remind me of disinfectant and cotton balls, and I've never once seen a pizza delivery dude I wanted to bang... and I order a lot of pizza! In addition, the background music is ridiculous. It sounds like the theme from *Sanford and Son* but with more sliding bass. Finally, porn doesn't work for women because the sight of a nude male body either makes us giggle or look away. You know how guys think we women turn off the lights when we make love because we're insecure about our bodies? We're not. We turn off the lights because we don't want to see yours. Keep this in mind the next time you think about suggesting we watch *Schindler's Fist* together.

Another fun Internet story involved the time the CEO of ComedyTime, an Internet comedy network, called me to say that a comedy clip of mine from a few years back had been posted and received an extremely high number of hits within the span of a day or two. Granted, I wasn't exactly crazy about the old set because it was filmed when I really wasn't doing much stand-up, and it featured an old routine I hadn't used for years.

ComedyTime was so thrilled with the reaction that they wanted me to do some work for them. I decided to check out the clip and made the mistake of reading the comments and message boards. Jesus lap-dancin' Christ, was it cold! I immediately regretted my decision to read all of the nasty, anonymously posted hatred; but in a sick way I couldn't stop. Geez, it was the cyber equivalent to giving myself little cuts. The comments were either gross and sexual (and those were the good ones) or really bitchy and negative, such as, "Women can't be funny"; "She's an airhead blonde"; "I hate her fake tits," etc. One of the positive comments said I looked like "the white Eva Longoria." I jumped all over that one; otherwise, I was absolutely devastated.

Fortunately, my brother Rick was visiting at the time of my message board bitch slap, and he was able to put things in perspective and make me feel better. Rick always makes me feel better. Rick and I have been inseparable since he came into this world, and we still call each other "pal." He is an outstanding human being whose passion is teaching, and he is beloved by his students. It should also be noted that Rick is a comedic genius, and is far funnier than I ever thought of being. This works for me because I can steal all his good material.

My brother explained how message boards were just one ladder rung above writing on public restroom walls, and shouldn't be taken to heart. Rick said that when two men go back and forth with some good old-fashioned bathroom graffiti trash talking, it's ever escalating. They swear at each other, accuse each other's mothers of engaging in horrible, lewd behavior, and accuse each other of performing unspeakable acts on dead animals, etc. This continues until someone eventually pulls the trigger and draws a picture of a penis. End game. The other guy's only move is to cross out the penis, but there really is no measured response. Apparently, you need to be the first dude to draw the penis. It's only a matter of how long you can hold out. Who knew? As per usual, Rick made me laugh my ass off, and I eventually forgot about all the creepy messages I had read.

I now subscribe to fabulous actress Edie Falco's philosophy. She says what people write about her is none of her business. Listen, if Tina Fey is susceptible to cyber swipes (see her 2009 Emmy speech), what hope do the rest of us mere mortals have? It's like when Halle Berry's and Uma Thurman's husbands cheated on them.

Important safety tip: don't google yourself. Ever. Even Kanye West isn't secure enough to handle that crap.

Along came Pauly

"Dude, I just got a new power drill that can penetrate the dense stream of conscious narrative of James Joyce."
—PAUL SCHMIDT

Throughout the years, I have held down a variety of jobs in various industries: flight attendant, television weather girl, interviewer of jockeys at a race track... By the way, have you ever met a real live jockey out in the wild? Cocky, horny little bastards. I mean they wear brightly colored silk outfits. Who else sports those besides members of the Ice Capades and Middle Eastern dudes in discos? They are very confident though. I guess it's because they're professional athletes, somewhat like NBA players who have been left in the dryer for far too long.

Whenever I would enter the locker room to interview the jockeys following a race, one would inevitably drop his towel and scream out something witty like, "Look at me, I'm a tripod!" And I would think to myself, "If I shove my earphones up your ass you'd be an iPod!" I think one brave soul once tried to go up on me, and I caught him shimmying up my leg like a little koala bear. I had to shake him off and put him out like a cigarette. It was very traumatic; I still can't watch *Seabiscuit* alone.

At any rate, my unorthodox career path has led to some great successes. I've also been fired so many times that I'm officially sanctioned by the NRA. My biggest vocational challenge came when I desperately wanted to leave the entertainment show I was hosting at a major Canadian network in order to do a comedy show. I realized how blessed I was to host a high profile national program of that ilk, but it really wasn't my soul's desire. Interviewing the celebrities was fine, but sitting rigidly behind a desk in a pastel suit and helmet hair while reading from a teleprompter was not my dream job whatsoever.

I fully understand that going from entertainment anchor to comedian is a quantum leap. You didn't see Nancy O'Dell in *The Aristocrats*, did you? And Mary Hart rarely does a tight ten-minute set at the Comedy Store.

However, I was determined to pursue my passion and several people were determined to see me fail. Fortunately, I had a champion at the network with whom I negotiated a new deal while she was flat on her back and I was wearing a black wig. Long story short: She was recovering from major back surgery, and it was Halloween. My contract was up so she invited me over to her home where we could discuss my future. I had decided to dress up as my natural hair color that year at the anchor desk for Halloween, and I didn't have the time to change. I thought this was all a very good portent for a career in comedy. I got my wish and began working on my own comedy-variety show.

A new kid called Paul had wondered over to our production offices and expressed a desire to work on the new show. Paul was really young and looked even younger—like a teenage version of Anson Williams (that was years ago and the guy still gets asked for ID every time we go out). I had never met Paul before, but later found out that he had seen me in the hallways of the television studio and had been terrified of me. Apparently, he was walking behind me once and my demeanor scared the living crap out of him. To be fair, it was during my short platinum blonde hair and pleather-Matrix outfit phase. Anyway, one day I walked into the boardroom where he was working with some of the other young members of our team on a raunchy sketch about a beloved, classic Canadian show called *The Littlest Hobo*, which featured the adventures of a brave German Shepherd.

To say that Paul was a tad shy back then would be like saying Courtney Love is a social drinker. I just remember his little cherubic face looking up at me while he quietly mumbled some joke he had written about the dog's "whoopsie hole." I laughed hysterically and immediately loved this adorable little dude. Whenever our executive producer would inquire who I wanted on a field shoot, I asked for Paul. We became fast buds.

The producers had hired an older male comic to help write

my opening monologues. This was not ideal. Although he was a great comedian and had been honing his chops in comedy clubs for years, our sense of humor and points of reference were vastly different. The material he wrote for me was completely inappropriate. With the day of our first show-taping fast approaching, it became quite apparent that I wouldn't be able to use any of the stuff the older guy had written for me, and so we decided to see what Paul was made of.

It was a Monday afternoon, and I was booked to do a comedy set at a local club that night. Our producer tracked down Pauly and told him to take a swing at creating a monologue that I could try out on the crowd that same evening. Paul had never written any stand-up in his life, and looked visibly shaken. He turned white. Well, he turned whiter (he's German).

This wunderkind delivered comedy gold that night, and Paul and I have been writing partners ever since. To date we've written a couple of comedy specials, several awards shows, two stage productions, many radio shows, a cartoon, and countless magazine articles together. Writing with Paul is truly one of my greatest joys on earth. It's seamless; and more often than not, we have no idea who wrote what. There's no ego, but there is a lot of goofing around. I don't know why the two of us work so well together. My guess is it's because Paul is wise beyond his years, brilliant, and has a great understanding of the female psyche; whereas I have the soul of a fifteen-year-old boy.

I wrote solo on this book and missed Paul dearly. This way though, I got to talk about him. Paul is my adopted brother, and definitely one of my angels. A German angel… See, anything's possible.

Chapter 12

The Panic Womb

(Desperate douche bags)

"Do or do not. There is no try."
—YODA

This is the final type of douche bag I will be exploring in detail. Of course, there are several other douches wandering the earth like evil versions of Kane from Kung Fu.

There are the (always annoying) passive aggressive douche bags. My advice? Whenever someone begins a sentence by saying, "Don't take this the wrong way but..." You must immediately flee the conversation. Nothing good is going to follow that waiver. Also, "Don't take this the wrong way but..." Can only be taken one way... up the butt!

There are cheap douchers who are frugal with their money and their love; but be careful not to confuse cheap with poor, especially in these troubling economic times. In fact, at one point my friend Kevin was so broke that I actually witnessed him reciting passages from the Bible and waving his hands over a pitcher of water in the desperate hope that it would turn into wine.

There are also bitter bags. Why become bitter? It's not satisfying, it's not attractive, and it's definitely not slimming. No experience, no matter how painful, is an excuse for anyone to reserve a table for one at the Bitter Bistro.

Look for some good in everything. There is an upside to every situation, even divorce. I don't know about you, but when my first husband and I ended our marriage, I became more desirable to him than a skanky ho at a Poison reunion concert. You know how make-up sex is always good? Well, divorce sex is like Space Mountain without the lineups. You just ride that mother as much as you can before the park closes. It's like driving a rental car. You can do whatever you want to it; drive the hell out of it, bang it up a little, spill drinks on the upholstery... Who cares? You're not keeping it. It's the next driver's problem.

There are jealous douche bags (the worst), poser douche bags (don't speak with a French accent and tell me what wine goes with oatmeal if you're from Detroit), etc., but there simply isn't enough time and space for all of the combinations and permutations of douches; and I'm growing tired of them.

Desperate douche bags are never coming from a place of power, and are generally harmless until their desperation becomes so extreme they resort to crazy and dangerous methods. We have all made the mistake of trying too hard, wanting something too much, or holding onto something with such a tight but clammy grip that it slips out of our hands. Desperate is never a good look because no one wants to be around a person who is sweating like Tom Sizemore before a urine sample. If you leave the house doused in Eau de Desperation, you will never attract anything (or anyone) positive.

Desperate douches are often cloying and eager to please. Desperadoes are far too quick to morph into whomever they are trying to impress. The desperate douche bag will sleep with someone far too quickly, eat far too much shit, and endure far too much abuse. Desperation often leads to depression, despair, and ultimately paralysis. The upside of desperation is that it can lead to drastic changes, which if channeled properly can be a driving force. Just simmer down first. Desperate douche bags just need to let go, relax, regain their power, and start looking for a picture of their dignity on the side of a milk carton.

Three redheads and a fake blonde

"I'm not offended by all the dumb blonde jokes because I know that I'm not dumb. I also know that I'm not blonde."
—DOLLY PARTON

I am not cool, I have never been cool, and barring a miracle like *goofy* and *hyper* becoming the new hip standard— I will never be cool. I am, however, somewhat wily (in a coyote getting blown-up kind of way) and savvy enough to surround myself with very cool people whom I observe and try to learn from.

Gingers have been getting a bad rap lately, mainly due to the cutting humor of *South Park* and the mere existence of David Caruso. But we all know that ginger women are red hot. There are three wonderful, powerful and very inspirational redheads in my life. These women are accomplished, generous and fearless. They lead their lives with gusto and do not suffer fools gladly. In fact, they do not suffer fools at all.

Tomasina is an unbeatable combination of Mexican fire and Irish sass. She is a tall and striking woman with long red hair, gorgeous, ample (real) breasts, and the most beautiful skin I've ever seen. I met Tomasina (aka: Tom) when I first began dating Ty. Tom and her husband Joey were dear friends of Ty's now-departed stepfather. Tom is Joey's second *and* fifth wife, and most definitely the love of his life. Ty was in attendance at their first nuptials.

After meeting Tom and Joey over lunch one day, they graciously invited Ty and me to join them at their beautiful villa in Zihuatanejo, Mexico. Although their place was absolute paradise, I must admit that I was initially very intimidated by Tom, and was convinced she hated me. I don't speak Spanish, and I felt as though my first trip to her home in Mexico was nothing but a festival of unintentional faux pas on my part. Tom even made me change the outfit I was wearing before she brought us to the charity bull fight she had organized, deeming my shirt far too revealing and expressing concern that my cleavage might distract a matador!

Four months later, this same woman walked me down the aisle at my wedding in Vegas. That's right; Ty and I were married in Vegas. You see, there are no windows or clocks in Vegas, so we had no idea we had only been together for seven months.

Tomasina's personality is larger than life, and her heart is even bigger. She is the most generous person I have ever met. She and her husband put up the money for our stage show, and they treat us like family whenever we are with them. She is my family here in the U.S.

The most extraordinary thing I came to learn about Tomasina is the fact that she has always put others first, and has always been magnanimous whether she has $10 to her name or $10 million.

Tomasina has a castle, a boat, and a matador's cape all named after her. Men will move mountains for her no matter how many times she changes her mind and decides that she wants to see what the mountains would look like in a different spot. They do this because she is a stunning woman, sure, but more importantly because she is always real and the first to laugh at herself. Now that's beauty that will move you.

I first met Belinda at a yoga class in Malibu. She was hard to miss. Belinda has alabaster skin, a ridiculously luxurious head of tousled crimson hair, and the body of death. Belinda's mother (who is now in her eighties) is a yoga instructor, and Belinda has a beautiful yoga practice. She is impossibly flexible and strong, and although I can't be entirely certain, I'm pretty sure she levitates. I would watch her flow from pose to pose and desperately try to emulate her. This mainly resulted in me crashing into the mirror or slightly injuring myself. I was like the yoga rodeo clown. I often fantasized that after Belinda finished yoga class, she would don a leather catsuit and fight crime.

One day I finally worked up the nerve to speak to her. I told Belinda it was very inspiring being next to her in yoga class... and very depressing. She tossed back her auburn mane and let out the most infectious laugh I've ever heard. She followed that up with a clever, witty comeback that included the word "dahling" delivered in a very sexy accent. Turns out, Belinda is from New Zealand where she was a big TV star. She had come to L.A. to try her hand at producing.

Belinda has become my closest confidant in L.A. I have a huge girl-crush on her, and I am still trying to copy her moves both on and off the yoga mat.

Some of Belinda's philosophies include being here in the now. She maintains that if you're happy in this moment, then remain present and enjoy it. If you dwell on the past, you're missing the point and deserve to be slapped. Belinda thinks that worry is like jealousy—useless, because it doesn't affect reality. She also believes that if someone asks for your opinion, you should really be honest and give it (without being mean). Be absolutely unafraid, and have the courage of your convictions. She also offers great advice to women on how to turn down requests: "If someone asks you to do something and it's just not possible for you to accommodate their wish, say no and then stop talking. Don't babble on giving excuses or trying to find ways to make it happen. I'm guilty of wanting to please everyone too dahling, but I don't see a lot of people scrambling to make me happy, so why do it?"

Women need to stop over processing everything and holding on to grudges. Grudge holding, says Belinda, takes an enormous amount of energy, and the grudges get heavier over time because they become soaked with bitter tears and dust mites.

She suggests that if it's recommended that we change our mattress every ten years because it's full of crap, then perhaps we should do the same with our psyches. She also proposes we raise our glasses and get over ourselves because, "Dahling, it could always be so much worse!" By the way, Belinda is also a gourmet cook. If I wasn't already taken, I think I would propose.

Laura is my vocal coach who has worked with many of the greats, including Elvis, Marilyn Monroe, Angie Dickinson... and the list goes on. I have no idea how old Laura is because she will never reveal her age (and strongly advises all women to keep that information under wraps). She is a tiny creature with a pile of shocking ruby hair resting atop her head; and she swears like a sailor. Laura is an accomplished singer and pianist. A true master, she has imparted so many incredible nuggets of wisdom to me that being in her presence and taking in her lessons is like finding the Holy Grail.

Laura's like Yoda with red hair. She endeavors to teach all of her students to "speak on the breath." According to Laura, if your voice has no breath, it has no soul. She is a stickler for proper pronunciation and abhors anything remotely resembling a nasal sound emanating out of your body. Laura says words are important because they are clothes for ideas. She taught me to linger on words beginning with *M*, *N* and *L* in order to create a good vibration.

She's all about standing up straight, shoulders back, stomach engaged, neck held high and sphincter relaxed (which is not as easy as it sounds). One time, Laura commanded me, "Speak from your tits!" I still don't know exactly what that means, but it made my husband a far better listener.

Laura will advise you to be sweet not nice, to smile with your eyes, and to never apologize. She cautions that no one should ever show their bottom teeth while talking or smiling, as it is very aging.

Laura encourages me to let the vulnerable part of me show on stage, and to live life on the edge of tears and laughter with the "give valve" wide open. Laura is magical and fascinating. She is one of the last, true broads.

Each one of these scarlet beauties lives a life of passion that is uncompromised, unapologetic, and most of all— unworried.

If you ignore it, it will come

"There are only two ways to live your life. One is as though nothing is a miracle. The other is as if everything is a miracle."
—ALBERT EINSTEIN

You never want to hear the words *desperate* and *dating* in the same sentence. They just don't work well together. It would be like pairing up Rosie O'Donnell and Donald Trump on the *Amazing Race*. I find dating fascinating; it's like an exotic animal in the jungle. I want to go live with it, observe its habits, learn its language, and better understand it—just like what Diane Fossey did with gorillas.

It's really interesting to return to the wacky world of dating after being married for nearly six years. The first thing I discovered when I was back in bachelorette mode, was who my target markets were. You know, the demographics that were attracted to me.

The first person who asked me out when I was single again was a nineteen-year-old Ultimate Fighting champion called Christian TKO (Total Knock Out). Now my girlfriends were all giving me the thumbs up and encouraging me to go for it, but I had to remind them that he was NINETEEN! For the love of Mary Kay Letourneau, his age started with a ONE. And the word *teen* was in there! I wouldn't know what to do or how to act because I've never taught school in Florida. Call me crazy, but I don't like to be the only one in the relationship who shaves. So apparently, one of my target markets is boy bands.

On the opposite side of the spectrum, I also discovered that old, loud white men also find me irresistible. I'm not kidding; I'm like sexual catnip to these guys. It got to the point where I was scared to walk by the CBS studios for fear that I would be gang-raped by the cast of *60 Minutes*.

I remember meeting an older gentleman on the beach in Malibu (old gentlemen are indigenous to Malibu). He appeared to be about 102-years-old, so naturally, he was wearing a thong. What happens to you men? Do you hit seventy-five and no longer care if your junk is hanging out? Do you just enjoy the challenge of painstakingly squeezing your boys into a tiny Speedo just so you can feel alive? This particular man had shocking white hair (on his head), and his body was all spotty and wrinkly. I swear to God, it was like watching John McCain in a banana hammock. This man fell for me hard and promised to take care of me for the rest of his life, which I roughly estimated at two weeks. Have you ever had someone look at you like you're number fourteen on the bucket list? It's like Yoda hitting on you: "Love you, I!" Plus old dudes try to be cool and hip, but they can't remain current for very long in any conversation. This grandpa told me he was a Howard Stern fan. Then he said he was on "The Facebook." After that minor slip, he just spiraled down and started talking about the hookers he and his buddy shared in Korea; then began naming all the silent film stars he had banged. "Talkies? They should have been called Screamies!" I politely turned him down, but encouraged him to audition for *Cocoon 3: Return to Denny's*.

Then a third group emerged: little people. It would seem that if there is a vertically-challenged man, a midget, or a Lilliputian within a fifty mile radius of me, they will come running over in a cloud of dust and suddenly appear next to me with their tongues hanging out like the Road Runner.

The other thing I discovered after years of being off the

market is that some things never change. I still morph into Jerry Lewis whenever I'm in the company of a man I really like and am attracted to. I become a total chat monster and make silly, over-exaggerated facial expressions, and am just a bow tie away from breaking into "Hoivin Cloivin, Nice Lady Helloi!"

The final thing I discovered about dating after divorce is that I had become a lightweight drinker. Unfortunately, I made this discovery during a date with a perfectly lovely, good-looking man. Apparently, my sass plus alcohol equals belligerence. By the end of the night, I was just barking out random commands at the poor guy: "Hey, take off your shirt! Lick my elbow! Do my roots!" No more tequila for me. I don't want to end up on YouTube again. After that incident, I decided I needed to find a safe house.

The most important thing I discovered was something I already knew—if you ignore it, it will come. Whenever you don't want anyone serious in your life, someone will show up on your doorstep faster than a Jehovah's Witness. Enter Ty. That's one of the biggest dating tips I can think of. Just let it go. Stay busy and stay focused on your own life. No one will complete you. That *Jerry McGuire* movie was bullshit. You need to become complete yourself first; then ideally, find another complete human to compliment you.

When we step back from someone, we leave them room to come closer.

Another tip is to be confident or to feign confidence, if necessary. It works with everyone all the time, no matter what age, race or gender. Why the hell do you think Prince is a sex symbol? I mean c'mon, he's five foot fuck-all and dresses like Anne Rice. Prince has been trying to grow in that same mustache for twenty-five years now. He's sexy because he's confident, and because of this Prince has been with some of the most beautiful women in the world. It could also be because he's obscenely rich, a rock star, and can dance better in ten-inch platform heels than most people can in flats... So maybe not the best example but you know what I'm getting at.

Don't date in fear. Even Winston Churchill said, "Courage is going from failure to failure without losing enthusiasm." Don't be too eager, don't hold on to anyone too tightly, and don't smother the object of your affection because it will kill him or her and then you will be single again. Most importantly, don't take yourself or dating so seriously. Avoid all desperate douche bags; and avoid being one.

CARE AND TREATMENT OF YOUR

Douche Bags

❱ Never humor or cater to douche bags as this will only encourage them.

❱ Do not attempt to deal with a crazy douche bag. Leave that to a professional.

❱ If an activity is douchy for you, plan to do something wonderful after the douche task is completed.

❱ Learn to separate the compulsory douchery from the optional.

❱ Remember to take douche bags in very small doses, and with plenty of water.

❱ Do not sink to a douche bag's level. Rise above it, and always take the douche high road.

❱ Do not live in fear. The real estate market is horrible there, and you're likely to live next door to a douche bag.

❱ Do not feed your douche bag after midnight.

❱ Make sure your douche bag flosses. It just seems like the right thing to do.

❱ Never let a douche bag get to you. Keep in mind that the douche bag was probably never picked by either side choosing teams in gym class.

❱ Remember people of all heights suffer from a Napoleonic complex.

❱ Do not shy away from calling a douche bag a douche bag.

❱ Don't drink and douche.

❱ Don't douche and drive.

❱ If someone you once cared for very much suddenly goes "rogue douche," try to focus on and remember the good times you once shared with them before they went over to the douche dark side.

❭ Try to see the humor in how your douche bag acts. Learn to treat these people as colorful characters in your life, and attempt to turn their doucheliciousness into hilarious anecdotes at parties.

❭ Keep in mind that when someone is negative or acting like a douche, it has nothing to do with you. Try to remain detached.

"I've been accused of vulgarity. I say that's bullshit."
—MEL BROOKS

I will leave you with this: Once during a Kabbalah class, the teacher explained to us the difference between a tourist mentality and a spy mentality. A tourist visits a new city or country and seeks out its beauty—the historic buildings, the breathtaking vistas, and the romantic places to eat. A spy enters a new city or country intent on finding everything that's wrong in that location. His mission is to uncover the weaknesses and flaws of the place. It would seem to me that we would all be a hell of a lot happier if we approached the people in our lives with a tourist mentality. It wouldn't hurt to approach ourselves that way either.

Please understand that the labeling of angels, vampires and douche bags is a terribly subjective art, and that one person's douche bag may very well be another person's angel. With the exception of Mother Teresa, Count Dracula and Hitler, every one of us has been an angel, vampire or douche bag at different times in our lives.

In all likelihood, each of us is a combination platter of all three. It's really just a matter of feeding your angel so that it will grow stronger, controlling your vampire so it doesn't control you, and kicking your douche right in the bag until you knock it out cold.

"And now here is my secret, a very simple secret: It is only with the heart that one can see rightly; what is essential is invisible to the eye."
—ANTOINE DE SAINT-EXUPÉRY